# HOLDING ON TO THE PROMISE

Women's Human Rights and the Beijing + 5 Review

*Edited by Cynthia Meillón
in collaboration with Charlotte Bunch*

Center for Women's Global Leadership
Rutgers, the State University of New Jersey

Holding on to the Promise:
Women's Human Rights and the Beijing + 5 Review

First Printing: May 2001

ISBN: 0-9711412-0-7

©Center for Women's Global Leadership
Rutgers, the State University of New Jersey
160 Ryders Lane
New Brunswick, NJ 08901-8555 USA
Ph: (1-732)932-8782
Fax: (1-732)932-1180
E-mail: cwgl@igc.org
Website: www.cwgl.rutgers.edu

Holding on to the Promise will be distributed by:
Women, Ink.
777 United Nations Plaza
New York, NY 10017
Ph: (1-212)687-8633
Fax: (1-212)661-2704
E-mail: wink@womenink.org
Website: www.womenink.org

Editor: Cynthia Meillón
Production Manager: Linda Posluszny

Design by Mary Ellen Muzio
Printed by Command Web Offset Co.

# Table of Contents

Acknowledgements . . . . . . . . . . . . . . . . . . . . . . . . . . . . . . . . . . .v

## Introduction

Beijing + 5:
Beginning and Ending with Women's Human Rights . . . . . . . . . . . . .2
*Cynthia Meillón*

## The Symposium

Introduction: Imagine a World . . . . . . . . . . . . . . . . . . . . . . . . . . .8
*Charlotte Bunch*

### Part I: Current Challenges in Women's Human Rights

Women 2000: The Future of Human Rights . . . . . . . . . . . . . . . . . . .13
*Mary Robinson*

Women's Economic, Social and Cultural Rights:
A Response to the Globalization Agenda . . . . . . . . . . . . . . . . . . . .23
*Piedad Córdoba*

We Want it Paid with Interest! . . . . . . . . . . . . . . . . . . . . . . . . . . . . .32
*Asma Jahangir*

The Achievements and Challenges of the
Women's Human Rights Movement . . . . . . . . . . . . . . . . . . . . . . . .37
*Florence Butegwa*

Let's Light Another Candle . . . . . . . . . . . . . . . . . . . . . . . . . . . . . . .44
*Abena Busia*

### Part II: Innovative Praxis

Section 1: Violence Against Women:
New Strategies for Confronting Discrimination and Abuse . . . . . . .46

Silence and Complicity: Unmasking Abuses of
Women's Human Rights in the Peruvian Health Care System . . . . .49
*Ivonne Macassi*

Confronting Violence Against Women in the Whole of Society . . . .54
*Duška Andric-Ruzicic*

Organizing for Sexual Rights:
The Namibian Women's Manifesto . . . . . . . . . . . . . . . . . . . . . . . . .60
*Elizabeth Khaxas*

Redefining and Confronting "Honor Killings" as Femicide .................... 66
*Nadera Shalhoub-Kevorkian*

The Tokyo Tribunal:
Confronting Rape and Sexual Violence as War Crimes ....................... 73
*Indai Sajor*

Commentary
Challenging Resistance to Women's Human Rights .......................... 79
*Sunila Abeyesekera*

Commentary
The Only Thing We're Asking for is Implementation ........................ 82
*Pierre Sané*

Death Fireworks ............................................................ 85
*Bojana Blagojevic*

**Section 2: Women's Economic Rights:
Challenging the Structures of Injustice** ...................................... 86

Using CEDAW to Fight for Women's Inheritance Rights ..................... 89
*Sapana Pradhan Malla*

African Women Refugees in the United Kingdom:
Organizing against Oppression .............................................. 96
*Sarah Mukasa*

Labor Rights with a Feminist Perspective:
Organizing with Workers in the Central American Maquila Industry ........... 102
*Olga Rivas*

Poverty in the Midst of Prosperity:
Organizing for Economic Rights in the United States ........................ 107
*Joy Butts*

Building a Culture of Women's Human Rights in Nigeria ..................... 114
*Ayesha Imam*

Breakthrough–Using Popular Culture to Raise Social Awareness ............... 121
*Mallika Dutt*

Commentary
Holding Both States and the Private Sector Accountable ..................... 123
*Pierre Sané*

Commentary
Making the Connections:
Using Women's Experiences to Link Human Rights Issues .................... 126
*Sunila Abeyesekera*

Fin de Milenio ............................................................ 129
*Claroscuro*

## Beijing + 5 Analysis

Taking Stock: Women's Human Rights Five Years After Beijing ...............132
*Charlotte Bunch*

CEDAW and Beijing + 5: Consolidating Women's Human Rights
or Backtracking on Commitments? ......................................140
*Cynthia Meillón*

Beijing + 5 and Violence Against Women ..................................147
*Lisa Clarke*

References to Trafficking in the Beijing + 5 Document .....................156
*Cynthia Meillón*

Beijing + 5: Respecting, Promoting and Protecting Women's Diversities .........163
*Lisa Clarke and Cynthia Rothschild*

Women's Economic Rights:
A Few Steps Forward and a Long Way to Go ..............................173
*elmira Nazombe*

Liberation ...........................................................183
*Abena Busia*

## Appendix

A. The Symposium Program ............................................185

B. Summary of Center for Women's Global Leadership's
   Beijing + 5 Activities ..............................................186

C. Women Prepare for the Beijing + 5 Review ............................189

D. Working Paper on a Human Rights Based Approach
   to the Beijing + 5 Review ..........................................194

# Acknowledgements

There are many people whose time, labor, analysis and life experiences contributed to the making of this book and to the events recorded in it. It is impossible to thank them all here. Many of those we would like to recognize are included in the lists on the program for the Symposium in the Appendix to this book.

We wish to thank especially all of the women, together with their organizations, who provided the testimonies at the Women 2000 Symposium: Joy Butts, Mallika Dutt, Ayesha Imam, Elizabeth Khaxas, Ivonne Macassi, Sapana Pradhan Malla, Sarah Mukasa, Olga Rivas, Nadera Shalhoub-Kevorkian, Duška Andric-Ruzicic, and Indai Sajor. We also wish to thank those who helped to prepare the testimonies and worked with us in other ways that contributed to the success of the symposium, and those who provided additional information and insights that greatly strengthened the material presented in the book. Among them are: Elena Arengo, Roxanna Carrillo, Shanti Dairiam, Liz Frank, Lynn Freedman, Susana T. Fried, Sandra Lanman, Ilana Landsberg-Lewis, Debra Liebowitz, Kathy Hall-Martínez, Elsa Stamatapoulou, Erhyu Yuan, and the staff at the Kensington Welfare Rights Union.

We wish to thank all of the Global Center staff, who provided ongoing (and, at times, round-the-clock) support throughout the demanding Beijing + 5 experience: Jewel Daney, elmira Nazombe, Diana Gerace, Lucy Vidal, Lisa Clarke, Mia Roman and Claudia Hinojosa. Most especially, we thank Linda Posluszny, who was both co-producer of the symposium and production manager for this book.

Cynthia Meillón  Charlotte Bunch
Editor  Executive Director

# Introduction

# Beijing + 5: Beginning and Ending with Women's Human Rights

Cynthia Meillón

IN 1995, DELEGATES FROM 189 COUNTRIES MET IN BEIJING, CHINA to participate in the United Nations Fourth World Conference on Women. The meeting, which is generally referred to as the Beijing Women's Conference, marked over twenty years of activism to win guarantees from governments that concrete measures would at last be taken to put an end to the unequal treatment women face in nearly every country and culture. The conference culminated in consensus agreement on the Beijing Declaration and the Beijing Platform for Action.

The wording of the Beijing documents was gradually shaped out of lengthy and sometimes contentious negotiations among governments, in which old patterns and traditions of discrimination against women were frequently challenged. Of the two, the Platform for Action (PFA) is by far the most important; its wording and content clearly reflect the influence of countless women who fought for decades to have discrimination against women officially recognized and addressed. The Beijing Platform builds on the work of the three previous world conferences on women (Mexico City, 1975; Copenhagen, 1980; and Nairobi, 1985), but it goes beyond them in asserting women's rights as human rights and in the specificity of commitments to action to ensure respect for women's rights.

The results of the Platform for Action have been far reaching. In countries where United Nations treaties and agreements carry the weight of law, women have been able to use the PFA to prod their governments to repeal legislation that worked against women. Even before the conference took place, women in some countries used the publicity surrounding Beijing to increase public awareness of women's unequal status in their societies. For a time, "Beijing" became practically a household word, synonymous with women's rights, since the media, for once, had turned its attention to a meeting on women's issues.

And in the midst of all the fanfare, something very real was achieved. The Platform for Action is the most comprehensive expression of governments' commitments to human rights for women and girls that has ever been produced. Divided into twelve "critical areas of concern," it identifies the most important sites of discrimination against women and outlines actions for change that are to be taken at the national and international levels.

At Beijing, it was decided that governments would meet again in five years' time to evaluate how much progress they had made toward implementing the PFA. This evaluation process, which would end with a Special Session of the UN General Assembly in June 2000, came to be known as the Beijing + 5 Review, or B + 5.[1]

## B + 5: Fighting for Implementation

In keeping with UN procedure, a formal document was developed for negotiation through preparatory sessions of the Commission on the Status of Women. This "Outcomes Document" (as it was called)[2] listed achievements and obstacles that governments experienced in trying to fulfill the promises they made in the twelve Critical Areas of Concern during the Beijing conference. It also contained an extensive set of actions and initiatives that were to be taken in order to improve implementation of the Platform. Many of these "actions" were hotly debated throughout the review process.

Women committed to achieving women's full human rights hoped to use Beijing + 5 to push for ways to speed up and strengthen implementation of the PFA. The Center for Women's Global Leadership (Global Center) and its allies planned to use the review as an opportunity to convince governments to commit to more concrete goals than were originally set out in the Platform for Action. In the year-and-a-half leading up to the Special Session, women's rights activists from around the world made their way to New York for the international Preparatory Meetings (PrepComs) and to the regional Beijing + 5 meetings that took place in Asia Pacific, Africa, Europe/North America, and Latin America. At all of the meetings, women held workshops on specific aspects of women's human rights. And as they had done at the regional meetings for the Beijing Conference, they grouped themselves into caucuses, drafted recommended language for amending the document, and lobbied governments to promote these changes at the UN sessions.

As the review progressed, it became clear that some governments were not willing to accept stronger measures aimed at implementing the Platform. In fact, some wanted to use the review to try to weaken the language of the PFA and to renege on areas of women's human rights that they did not want to support. It was in this climate of uncertainty that we entered the final phase of the Beijing + 5 negotiations in June 2000.

**Focusing on Women's Organizing**

We invite you to think of this book as a mosaic. It does not attempt to tell the whole story of Beijing + 5, nor does it provide a detailed analysis of all the views presented there. It does, however, provide a series of snapshots that reflect much of the work carried out by the Center for Women's Global Leadership and the international network of like-minded organizations and individuals who work together to promote and protect women's human rights. It also highlights some of the ways women are organizing for their human rights, which was a theme of primary importance throughout the process.

The book is divided into two sections. The first contains a series of speeches and presentations from a human rights symposium that was organized by the Global Center on the eve of the UN Special Session. "Women 2000: A Symposium on Future Directions for Human Rights" was designed to provide a rallying point for women before entering the final stage of the Beijing + 5 process. Over 1,300 people attended the six-hour event, which was held at Columbia University. In order to encourage maximum participation, simultaneous translation in Spanish, French, and English was provided. A gallery adjacent to the theater was filled with information tables from over seventy human rights groups and related organizations. A spirit of combat filled the hall as speakers reminded the audience of the need to enter the UN negotiations with audacity, courage, and commitment to defending the gains women made at Beijing.

Although it had always been foreseen that the Global Center would organize a public event just prior to the opening of the UN Special Session, it now seemed more necessary than ever to hold a meeting where women could reaffirm their commitment to women's human rights in a way that would make governments fully aware that we were not prepared to accept backtracking or postponement of the commitments made at Beijing. Although the structure of the symposium resembled that of the human rights tribunals the Global Center had facilitated at the UN world conferences of the 1990s, it differed in a very significant way: Rather than hearing testimony about cases of abuse, the audience was presented with specific examples of how women are using the tools available to them (and in some cases, inventing new ones) to organize locally, regionally and globally to demand and defend their human rights.

The symposium brought together women's human rights activists who are doing innovative organizing work in their own countries. Their testimonies served to illustrate, not only the tremendous amount of creativity with which women are addressing human rights issues, but also new and emerging trends in human rights abuses internationally. The presentations were preceded by keynote speeches by women whose commitment to human rights goes back many years, which provided an overview of the achievements and the current state of the movement for women's human rights.

For this publication, the testimonies and speeches have been edited and annotated in order to make them as accessible as possible. They are not presented in the exact order they were given, but are grouped into two thematic areas. The first deals with specific instances of violence against women that are currently taking place. The second looks at violations of women's economic rights and the structural underpinnings that give rise to injustice in societies. Each set of presentations is followed by commentary which links the testimonies to broader issues and trends in human rights today.

The symposium was interspersed with poetry and music by women who are using art to educate and inspire on issues of women's human rights. Examples of their work have also been reproduced in this book.

**Counting Our Losses and Gains**
The second section of the book deals specifically with the Beijing + 5 Outcomes Document. It contains papers by members of the Global Center staff that look at the results of the review negotiations in five areas: the treatment of the Convention on the Elimination of All Forms of Discrimination against Women (CEDAW); violence against women; trafficking in women; respecting women's diversities; and economic justice and women's economic rights.

We have chosen to focus on these particular areas because they are fundamental to women's human rights and because they form an important part of the Global Center's work in general, as well as during the Beijing + 5 process. Although written by individuals, the analysis is a collectively evolving work, shaped through our advocacy experiences and our ongoing dialogue with women around the world. The papers are preceded by an essay by Charlotte Bunch that takes an overall look at the Beijing + 5 process. We hope this section will prove useful to readers who are interested in working with the content of the document itself.

Following these two sections, an appendix to the book contains copies of documents related to the Global Center's work during Beijing + 5, including the *Working Paper on a Human Rights Based Approach to the Beijing + 5 Review*, which was prepared for use throughout the review process. A program from the Women 2000 symposium has been included, along with a list of other activities organized by the Global Center in the period leading up to the Special Session.

**Women as Winners**

As the Beijing + 5 review progressed, it became apparent that, despite the difficulties encountered, probably the richest aspect of the process was the way in which women from around the world were able to work together. The Coalition for the Beijing Platform brought together over 500 women's organizations in an effort to hold onto the gains that were made at Beijing. Throughout the process, numerous workshops, panels and group lobbying efforts were carried out by teams that were strongly international in their make up. The experience was greatly enriched by the presence of a large number of young women who participated in the Youth Caucus, in their regional caucuses, and as members of the thematic caucuses.

While the Beijing Conference showed the world that an international women's human rights movement existed, Beijing + 5 proved that it has remained intact and continues to grow stronger and more diverse. This may be the most important lesson we have learned from the experience, and the one that will best serve us in the future.

# Notes

1. For more information about the Beijing + 5 process, see Appendix C, *Women Prepare for the B + 5 Review* by Susana Fried and Charlotte Bunch.

2. The final version of the Beijing + 5 document is titled *Report of the Ad Hoc Committee of the Whole of the twenty-third special session of the General Assembly*. Throughout the negotiations, however, the document was called *Further actions and initiatives to implement the Beijing Declaration and Platform for Action, Proposed Outcomes*, and generally referred to as the "Outcomes Document." The document can be viewed at the website: http://www.un.org/womenwatch/confer/beijing5/.

# The Symposium

# Introduction:
# Imagine a World

*Charlotte Bunch*

WE PLANNED THIS EVENT ON THE EVE OF THE UN GENERAL Assembly Special Session to review the Beijing Fourth World Conference on Women, in order to highlight the gains women made in Beijing and to provide an opportunity to look at women's organizing around the world based on the recognition of women's rights as human rights—a recognition that was achieved during the past decade.

We invited panelists to open this session by reflecting on the achievements and challenges in women's human rights over the last ten years. They will look at the UN world conferences leading up to Beijing that took place in Rio (Earth Summit), Vienna (Human Rights), Cairo (Population and Development), and Copenhagen (Social Summit)—as well as at Beijing—and perhaps more importantly, reflect on the work of women everywhere at the grassroots. We have asked the speakers to discuss the challenges ahead in seeking to make human rights a lived reality for all women and girls. This opening panel is followed by ten examples of "innovative praxis"—work being done at the local level to bring human rights concepts and instruments to the daily struggles of women. Each of the presenters tells us about the violations of women's human rights they are addressing and the strategies they have adopted to end those abuses.

*Charlotte Bunch is Executive Director of the Center for Women's Global Leadership.*

We have also asked two leading advocates for the human rights of women to provide commentary after both sets of presentations in order to put these concrete local experiences in a broader context and to focus on what this tells us about the work that lies ahead in the next decade. More specifically, they will also look at what this means with regard to the United Nations Special Session, or Beijing + 5, and what the UN and governments ought to be doing and saying this coming week if they are serious about advancing women's human rights.

Given what has been happening in the endless negotiations over the last six months and the state of those negotiations on the eve of this Special Session, it seems that this symposium is needed even more than we had originally anticipated. For in spite of the commitments that governments made in Beijing to advance the human rights of women and girls in many areas—from education and the economy to violence against women, health, and decision-making—there seems to be reluctance on the part of many governments to set more specific goals and targets, and to commit real resources to the actual implementation of those words—those hard won words—that represent the work of hundreds of thousands of women in the Beijing process.

What we need, in the phrase of the Latin American NGOs at their regional meeting to prepare for Beijing + 5, which was held in Lima, Peru in February, is *algo más que palabras*. More than words, we need actions.

Instead, what has been happening in this preparatory process is that good proposals that have been made for action—many of which are supported by some of the governments—are being diminished, one by one, with the addition of phrases like "where appropriate." Or, instead of "adopting," they say "consider adopting." Also, specific dates and numerical targets are being removed or questioned, often by only a handful of very vocal delegates determined to weaken the document.

One of the clearest examples of this weakening was the proposal to change the call in the Beijing + 5 "Outcomes Document" for the repeal of all legislation that actually legally discriminates against women. We know there is a lot of legislation that has been passed to end discrimination that is not implemented, but I am talking about actual laws that are discriminatory. In the original draft, there was a call to repeal all such laws by the year 2005. If you consider that 165 countries have already pledged to do so by signing the Convention on the Elimination of All Forms of Discrimination against Women (CEDAW), 2005 is already too late for something that should have been done in the last century. Nonetheless, when there was a proposal to call for repealing such legislation by 2005, someone asked to insert the words "as soon as possible" instead of the date. In the final document, this sentence now says that governments are to review legislation "with the view to striving to remove discriminatory provisions as soon as possible, preferably by 2005."

Now, I ask you, as human rights activists, how do we monitor and hold governments accountable to "as soon as possible?" Of course, we would all say "as soon as possible," or at least "as soon as necessary" has already passed. So when is "as soon as possible?" And that is the question we must emphasize; to hold governments accountable, we need specific commitments to targets and goals that can be measured. With this type of wording, we must convince governments that "as soon as possible" must be now. It is not five years from now. It is not ten years from now. It is now.

This is the point where this process must be engaged, because some countries are seeking to undermine human rights and the Beijing Platform, not by directly attacking it, but by these kinds of subtle adjectives and slight diminutions of the words that are there. And in doing so, they have also been resisting the international monitoring of their human rights commitments and practices—the international monitoring that is at the heart of the United Nations human rights system.

The reluctance to use human rights concepts and instruments in this review process has also been disturbing. Even the mention of the Women's Convention has been challenged. References to the Women's Convention and its Optional Protocol have been deleted or diminished in many places and references to other human rights instruments of the United Nations system—to all the other treaties to which women have a right—have been eliminated from this document. The human rights underpinning of this document, which was so strong in Beijing, is being gradually whittled away, not with a direct assault to eliminate it, but by slowly making it weaker.

There has been agreement in the Political Declaration for the Beijing + 5 Review that the Beijing Platform for Action is to be reaffirmed. This is a very important success, and governments have stated that they have the responsibility to work to implement it. Nevertheless, a handful of countries continue to drag the process down, to stall, and to keep inserting phrases aimed at watering down the commitments that were made in Beijing. We must demand that they no longer hold this document hostage. Over the next five days, we must insist that a strong, action-oriented document that does not go back on Beijing commitments, that upholds the integrity of the Beijing Platform for Action, and that moves forward the necessary steps to implement it must emerge from this process.

In this symposium and in other NGO activities during this week, women will demonstrate that we are moving ahead—that women are working to implement the Platform for Action and to realize the human rights of women locally, nationally, regionally and internationally, in spite of obstacles that have been put in our path. In spite of challenges and obstacles from globalization to fundamentalist backlash, women have become a global force for change that will transform this century, and we will not be turned back. We will move forward. This is the message that we hope will be transported from these halls to the halls of the United Nations tomorrow morning when the Special Session begins. We hope this event will add to and strengthen the resolve of the many delegates there who are committed to preserving the integrity of the Beijing Platform and to working to advance women's human rights.

In this symposium, we bring you a taste of the future, of what women and committed men are doing, and of what we think governments should be looking at and reviewing if they want to have a serious Beijing + 5 Review. We hope this event inspires and informs you as we share reflections, discuss challenges, and imagine a world where all women and girls enjoy their human rights.

*Part I:*
*Current Challenges in Women's Human Rights*

# Women 2000: The Future of Human Rights

Mary Robinson

THIS IS AN ESPECIALLY IMPORTANT WEEK FOR THE CAUSE OF women's human rights. The Beijing Plus Five Special Session can be another milestone on the road to women's achieving full legal, social, economic and political equality. The content of the discussion over the coming week has long term implications and will shape the debate for the immediate future. Women all over the world will follow the work of the Beijing Plus Five review closely and will be counting on those involved to play a constructive role in advancing the cause of women's rights. What the last three years have brought home to me vividly is the stark inequalities in women's and girls' life choices in our so-called "global village." At times the gap seems to be one of centuries, so we have a lot to do.

The Beijing Plus Five Review provides the opportunity to hold meetings and roundtables such as this one. These meetings offer the possibility to share experience and plan strategies and, in that way, to make the discussions about Beijing Plus Five a genuinely participatory and productive process. The contributions of the panel members and the testifiers from different regions will provide us with valuable good practices that will help our work in the Office of the High Commissioner for Human Rights.

I would like to pay tribute to the Center for Women's Global Leadership, and to Rutgers University for organizing this event, and indeed to Columbia

*Mary Robinson is the United Nations High Commissioner for Human Rights.*

University, with which I have some connection, for co-sponsoring and providing the venue. This event, and all the work that goes into it, shows once again the enormous contribution of the Center for Women's Global Leadership. I know it is always invidious to single out an individual, but I have a rare opportunity which I intend to take, to pay a personal tribute to Charlotte Bunch. I have much admired, most of all, her vision and her passion for change, which I think personify the role of the Center for Women's Global Leadership.

## The Future of Human Rights

First, a word about the future of human rights. I believe we are at a critical stage in the development of human rights. The interest in human rights as an issue has become universal. I doubt if there has been a time when the subject has been so widely referred to or written about, or when it has been accorded so key a role in political and economic debate. Major advances have been and are being made on the legislative front. I think for example, of the Optional Protocol to CEDAW[1] and the two Optional Protocols to the Convention on the Rights of the Child.[2] I think, too, of important recent decisions, such as the decision to appoint a Special Representative of the Secretary General to implement the UN Declaration on Human Rights Defenders. I think of the evidence of strengthened interest in economic, social and cultural rights as seen in the appointment by the Commission on Human Rights, at its latest meeting, of special rapporteurs on the right to food and the right to housing.

Yet, even as we welcome these testimonies to the growing prominence of human rights, we inevitably come up against the many instances where rights continue to be gravely abused and where progress seems to be slow or non-existent. The challenge we face is to keep up the pressure on governments and those in positions of power to honour the undertakings they have made in the name of human rights.

## Women's Human Rights

How do I see the future for women's human rights? The chief message I would like to convey today is, in the words of the Beijing Declaration, that the human rights of women and the girl child are an inalienable, integral and indivisible dimension of universal human rights. The principles of equality and non-discrimination have been central pillars of the human rights movement and of the United Nations system from the Charter onwards. These principles are at the core of human rights treaties, covenants, and declarations. They have been reiterated at numerous conferences, most notably at Beijing and Vienna. The responsibility of governments is also clearly defined. It is to achieve full and equal enjoyment by women of all human rights—economic, social and cultural, as well as civil and political—and the full participation of women as both agents and beneficiaries of development.

It is clear, as we look at women's situations around the world, that progress falls far short of the goals we seek. If we consider the crucial issue of violence against women, we are faced with the stark fact that women continue to be victims of violence in all its manifestations. Violence, both physical and psychological, is regularly inflicted on many women and is manifested throughout the life cycle. In situations of conflict and of gross human rights violations, women are particularly vulnerable targets. There is a special burden of responsibility on governments to protect women from rape, abduction, and other forms of gender-based violence, but it is a duty which is all too often neglected or ignored.

I remember a fifteen-year-old girl whom I met in Cambodia. She explained that her parents had sent her to Phnom Penh for a job in a factory. But that wasn't what happened. She was taken into a brothel and compelled to work eighteen hours a day in sex work—very violent sex work—until she escaped and came to the small center where I met her. I sat with a number of young girls last June in Sierra Leone, all of whom had been raped, and raped again after the rebels had invaded Freetown. And as they told their individual stories, each of them broke down. They cried, but in fact, they were beginning to heal. And what was incredibly moving was that one of them had her school uniform on, and she was going that day to face an exam. And I thought, "the resilience that shows, the courage, the possibilities, once there is support there, to try to put a terrible experience behind one." But also, the background of such terrible violence. The report just issued by UNICEF, *Domestic Violence Against Women and Girls* brings home the scale and persistence of that problem worldwide.[3]

Violence of another kind is perpetrated against millions of women who are deprived of access to political and economic rights and power. Women are routinely barred from enjoying equal participation in public life and are denied access to equal education and proper healthcare, especially in relation to their reproductive rights. The report on *The World's Women 2000* produced by the United Nations Statistics Division concluded starkly that "Women remain at the lower end of the segregated labor market and continue to be concentrated in a few occupations, to hold positions of little or no authority, and receive less pay than men."

For the Beijing Plus Five Review to be successful, it must address these failings and come up with innovative strategies to implement full equal rights for women. The legal base is there in the principles of equality and non-discrimination which form an integral part of international law, and the standards have been set out in detail in the Beijing Declaration and Platform for Action. The challenge is to implement these agreed standards in practice.

Before considering what results we can hope for from the Beijing Plus Five Review, I would like to mention two areas of particular present concern: the rise in trafficking and the gender dimension of racism and racial discrimination.

## Trafficking

The problem of trafficking in persons has become so acute that it is finally attracting the level of international attention it merits. Contributory factors include the growing disparity in wealth in societies and the disproportionate percentage of women among those living in poverty. Globalization and the revolution in communications also play a part, as do the troubles being experienced by economies in transition. Conflicts, whether internal or international, are breeding grounds for trafficking. The presence of military personnel in conflict situations, even in a peace-keeping capacity, can be a further aggravating factor.

Crucially, it is now understood that, because of the core elements of coercion and exploitation, trafficking constitutes violence against women and consequently a violation of their basic rights.

Devising effective methods of combating trafficking has not been easy and success to date has been limited. What is required is a consistent approach, based on a shared understanding of the problem. Trafficking is not a single event but a series of constitutive acts and circumstances implicating a wide range of actors. There are health, security, economic, and immigration issues involved. Those who control trafficking are ruthless and persistent, many with close links to organized crime.

Anti-trafficking measures must take account of these multiple dimensions to the problem. They must address the entire cycle of trafficking, starting with improvements in the information base, ensuring an adequate legal framework and effective law enforcement, preventative measures, protection and support for trafficked persons and coordinated national, regional and international responses. And the root causes of trafficking must be addressed, such as poverty, inequality and discrimination.

Within the United Nations system, an increasing number of Treaty Bodies and Special Mechanisms of the Commission on Human Rights have been focusing attention on the issue of trafficking and making recommendations. A number of Special Rapporteurs have addressed the problem in the context of their respective mandates. I would particularly draw your attention to the latest report by the Special Rapporteur on Violence against Women, Radhika Coomaraswamy.[4]

The fight against trafficking is a high priority for my Office. We are working actively towards the integration of human rights into the legal and policy aspects of international, regional, and national trafficking initiatives. We are carrying out projects in the Balkans and in Asia. I place particular emphasis on cooperation with organizations such as the Council of Europe, the United Nations Development Program and the International Organization of Migration, and to the channeling of funds to NGOs through the United Nations Trust Fund on Contemporary Forms of Slavery. It is at the grassroots level that this problem is going to really be addressed, but people at the grassroots level need the kind of help that I've been outlining.

Trafficking in persons is a priority because it is a compelling human rights issue, an infringement of a whole spectrum of fundamental rights which has reached global proportions. Trafficking is the very antithesis of the Universal Declaration of Human Rights and the struggle to eliminate it represents one of the toughest human rights challenges in the world today.

**Gender Dimension of Racism**
Another aspect of women's rights which I feel calls for close attention is the gender dimension of racism. This subject has particular relevance as we prepare for the World Conference against Racism, Racial Discrimination, Xenophobia and Related Intolerance, which will be held in South Africa next year, from August 31 to September 6, 2001. The Beijing Declaration and Platform for Action recognized that "many women face additional barriers to the enjoyment of their human rights because of such factors as their race, language, ethnicity, culture, religion, disability or socio-economic class or because they are indigenous people, migrants, displaced women, or refugees. They may also be disadvantaged and marginalized by a general lack of knowledge and recognition of their human rights as well as by obstacles they meet in gaining access to information and recourse mechanisms in cases of violation of their rights."

The Beijing wording is useful because there is a tendency to speak of so-called "double discrimination" in relation to women of a racial or ethnic group who experience discrimination based both on their gender and on their race or ethnicity. But in real life the problem is far more complex than this. There are, in fact, multiple potential forms of discrimination involved.

A gender analysis of racial discrimination recognizes that racial discrimination does not affect men and women equally, or in the same way. To promote and protect the rights of all persons to be free from racial discrimination, it is necessary to ensure the rights of women when they are similarly situated to men and when they are not. There are circumstances in which women suffer racial discrimination of a different kind or to a different degree than men, or in which discrimination primarily affects women.

To understand the problem, we need to consider what forms violations take, the context in which they occur, the consequences of a violation, and the availability and accessibility of remedies to victims. This is work that has not yet been done, and we've just got to do it. I look to you to help us to do this in preparation for the World Conference against Racism.

**The form:** One can ask what is the nature of the particular injury, infringement, or obstacle experienced by a victim because of race, gender, or race and gender? For example, women of a particular racial or ethnic group may be the victims of trafficking or sexual slavery. Or, as we have seen in many recent conflicts, women of particular ethnic or religious groups may be targeted for sexual abuse.

**The context:** In what legal or practical situation or context does gender-based racial discrimination or race-based gender discrimination or sexual abuse occur? For example, a particular racial or ethnic group of women may face added discrimination where there are inadequate labour laws and safety standards to protect them.

**The consequences of the violation:** What are the consequences or impact of violations experienced by victims due to their gender and/or race? In racial and ethnic conflicts, women who are sexually abused due to their ethnicity or race often become pregnant as a result. In many countries, there are social or legal barriers to women who seek redress for rape or sexual abuse, thus adding to their suffering.

**The availability and accessibility of recourse procedures and remedies:** To what extent does race and/or gender limit or act as a barrier to recourse procedures and remedies? Illiteracy, lack of resources, restriction on access to public places and lack of legal standing, amongst other barriers, may act as limits to women members of particular racial or ethnic groups.

There are also distinct forms of discrimination which occur when race and gender factors intersect or compound one another. The position of girls and female youth is an example. They may face discrimination, not only on the basis of gender and race, but because of another vulnerability—their age.

Clearly, the gender dimensions of racial discrimination are complex and varied. Yet, this very complexity requires the attention of the UN member States, national institutions, civil society and the United Nations in order to address the problem. A fundamental first step is to gather better information on the lives of the women and girl children in our world. There are major gaps in the information available to us. The next step, after compilation and analysis of information, is the putting in place of policies and programmes that will ensure the full equal enjoyment of rights by women and girls. Such reports as we have indicate that there are few laws, policies or programes which deal specifically with the rights of women who are in an additionally disadvantaged position due to racial or ethnic discrimination, xenophobia, or racial intolerance.

What is certain is that many women experience multiple discrimination and the question ought to be examined in depth. The issue of the gender dimension of racism and racial discrimination is on the agenda of the World Conference against Racism, and I intend to ensure that it receives proper consideration at the conference.

**Beijing Plus Five**

As I said at the outset, the week ahead has particular significance for the future of women's human rights. I see the main challenge as being to consolidate the achievements of Beijing, to move the agenda forward in practical ways and to assess if governments have honoured their commitments.

I would draw your attention to the paper which my Office has circulated for the Beijing Plus Five Review Conference, called *Building on Achievements: Women's Rights Five Years after Beijing.*[5] The paper examines the basic principles and standards applying to women's rights and addresses a number of key issues, including reproductive health rights, gender equality and property, land rights and inheritance, gender equality and the family, and trafficking.

As well as these overriding considerations, there are a number of specific outcomes I would like to see from this week's discussions:

1. No dilution of the Beijing Declaration and Platform for Action; the human rights standards agreed at Beijing and Vienna must be maintained.
2. States must assume the primary responsibility for ensuring women's equal rights. But they must recognize that theirs is part of an integrated response which calls for the full participation of civil society, including

NGOs. All States should ratify CEDAW and the Optional Protocol and do so without reservations.

3. While national, cultural, religious, and historical considerations are important and must be respected, they can never be allowed to be used as justifications for the infringement of women's human rights.
4. Due attention should be paid to the economic, social and cultural rights of women. Poverty is linked to many human rights abuses which affect women's lives and is one of the main factors in migration, trafficking, and forced labour. The moral obligation on the developed countries to transfer resources to those living in poverty is as great as ever in the modern globalized world.
5. The gender perspective should be mainstreamed into all human rights activities of governments and the United Nations system. Gender equality is not separate from other rights; it is an overarching principle that applies to the enjoyment of all rights. Mainstreaming gender acknowledges the different ways in which gender roles and gender relations shape women's and men's access to rights, resources and opportunities at all stages of the life cycle. But it must be genuine mainstreaming, not merely data collection or rhetoric.
6. The contribution and courage of human rights defenders should be recognized. Women human rights defenders face particular risks and dangers, especially when the rights they protect relate to issues of sexuality and reproductive rights. Diversity and its link to human rights must be respected.

It is fitting that I refer to human rights defenders at an event organized by Rutgers University, since it was Rutgers University Press which published the fine collection of women's writing on human rights entitled *A Map of Hope*.[6] I said in the foreword to that book, "Fighting for women's rights is a positive struggle which recognizes the quality of a women's contribution to every aspect of the life of the community: politics, industry, commerce, education, academic life, agriculture, the home." I believe that we should always bear that in mind as we champion women's human rights. Women are true peacemakers and peace-builders in war-torn and divided societies everywhere. A society which denies women their rights can never claim to have attained full human rights. One which embraces women's equal rights, on the other hand, will fulfill the vision of a democratic society and will ensure peace, security, and sustainable development for all its people.

I believe that we should always bear in mind, as we champion women's human rights, that women are the resource of this century. We have heard before that this is going to be the century of the participation of women. I have to say that the last three years have convinced me of the incredible wisdom of that. If you look at societies where women are participating, they are democratic and they are making good development progress. If you look at countries where women are not allowed to play their full part, there are multiple problems in that society. So part of what we have got to do is get the message across that the future for all our countries and all our traditions and societies is much better when women can play their full part—when they can access the resources and empower themselves to use their full skills and energies. My map of hope is to look at the century and see the potential of women and know that early in it we have this review to galvanize our strengths, to give the signal to millions of women who are watching and listening. And they are, believe me. They are watching and listening to what is happening this week, and it is up to us to give them the positive message and to ensure that governments adopt a forward looking document that builds on what was gained five years ago in Beijing.

# Notes

1. CEDAW is the abbreviation commonly used to refer to the Convention on the Elimination of All Forms of Discrimination against Women, sometimes called the Women's Convention. The convention entered into force on September 3, 1981. The Optional Protocol to CEDAW is an additional formal instrument, separate from the CEDAW convention, that introduces a procedure whereby the Committee on the Elimination of Discrimination Against Women (called the CEDAW Committee) can receive and investigate complaints of cases of discrimination against women, including those brought forth by individuals, in countries that have ratified both CEDAW and the Optional Protocol. The Optional Protocol was adopted on December 19, 1999. At the time of this writing, there is a campaign aimed at convincing a greater number of member states to sign it.

2. The Convention on the Rights of the Child was adopted by the UN in 1989. It is noteworthy for being the first legally binding international instrument to incorporate the full range of human rights—civil and political rights and economic, social and cultural rights. There are two Optional Protocols to the Convention: The Optional Protocol on the involvement of children in armed conflict, and the Optional Protocol on the sale of children, child prostitution and child pornography.

3. UNICEF. *Domestic Violence Against Women and Girls. Innocenti Digest* No. 6 (May 2000). Available at: http://www.unicef-icde.org/pdf/domestic.pdf.

4. *Integration of the Human Rights of Women and the Gender Perspective: Violence Against Women,* E/CN.4/2000/68/Add.2, 8 February 2000. Available at: http//:www.unhcr.ch/huridocda/huridoca.nsf/.

5. *Building on Achievements: Women's Rights Five Years after Beijing,* Office of the United Nations High Commissioner for Human Rights, May 2000. Available at: http://www.unhchr.ch/html/menu2/contirbeijing.htm.

6. Marjorie Agosín (ed.), *A Map of Hope: Women's Writing on Human Rights,* (Piscataway, New Jersey: Rutgers University Press, 1999).

# Women's Economic, Social and Cultural Rights: A Response to the Globalization Agenda

Piedad Córdoba

WOMEN'S HUMAN RIGHTS ARE INCLUDED IN THE FRAMEWORK of universal human rights. This simple and rather obvious affirmation contains a profound contradiction. It is a clear example of the condition of inequality that has historically kept women down and that is only now beginning to enter the collective consciousness of the male-centered world.

Why is it necessary to speak of women's human rights when it should be enough simply to speak of "human rights?" Since we are human beings, all enshrined principles, treaties, conventions and norms apply to women. Nevertheless, we know that this has not historically been the case, which is why we have to resort to specific standards and interpret, analyze and fight to have human rights instruments extended to women.

Neither the Universal Declaration of Human Rights[1] nor the International Covenant on Economic, Social and Cultural Rights,[2] which are among the principal instruments of international human rights law, make a distinction between the rights of men and the rights of women. These documents only refer to persons. But the biased application in benefit of men has given rise to women's primary struggle—to reach a place where political, economic, and social institutions do not limit the application of human rights to only one half of society.

*Piedad Córdoba is a Senator of the Republic of Colombia and a women's human rights activist.*

Without this distortion in human rights coverage—which can be explained by the fact that structures and institutions have been built around men and therefore exclude everybody else—there would be no need for an instrument like the Convention for the Elimination of All Forms of Discrimination against Women (CEDAW).[3] The fact that about twenty years ago a Convention of this type was opened for ratification—and it is considered to be one of the greatest achievements in favor of equality to date—is the best evidence we have of the profound distance that separates men and women from the benefits of development.

**Laws Are Not Enough**

It cannot be denied that formal *de jure* equality between men and women exists in nearly every country, particularly in Latin America. In addition to ratification of the instruments of international law, national legislation in the countries of the region contains laws on equal opportunity. Laws, however, are not enough, and this is clearly illustrated when we look at the gender breakdown of statistics on development produced by such bodies as the United Nations. We have a long way to go to if we are to move beyond the liberal-bourgeois equality of today—in which we are all equal before the law—to a democratic socialist equality which incorporates favorable treatment for people with disadvantages. There are many social differences—sex, race, economic position, to name a few—that lie completely outside a person's control and that justify different treatment and a greater commitment on the part of the state. For example, some people have access to the economic means that are necessary in order to live with dignity, while others—who do not—live in poverty.

The problem, therefore, centers not in an absence of laws but in the weak, and at times non-existent, political will to fulfill the international commitments that governments have made and in the absence of processes for bringing about complete and fully integrated change in favor of human rights. This is true in relation to civil and political rights and even more so with regard to economic, social and cultural rights, in which the inequalities are even more marked.

This lack of political will to guarantee women equality of opportunity so that we can access development owes much to the notion that the economic, social and cultural rights are to be applied gradually or deferred till a later time because they require the allocation of resources, which are nearly always scarce and are not always invested in a way that gives priority to such commitments. However, this does not mean that the essential element of respect for these rights need be absent. And when respect for such rights falls below a certain minimum, the state party is in violation of its obligations. All too often, when states do not even guarantee that minimum of respect, they defend themselves by saying that they lack the resources to fulfill their obligations toward women. Even a brief analysis of the International Covenant on Economic, Social and Cultural Rights—which has been around since 1966—brings this home. The rights are recognized and the obligations to adopt concrete measures are clear, but public policies do not respond to either.

The first part of the Covenant states that all peoples have the right to self-determination and to freely dispose of their wealth and resources, and that they cannot be deprived of their means of subsistence.

In the second part of the Covenant, reference is made to states' commitments to put economic, social and cultural rights into practice. It establishes that they must assign the maximum possible resources in order to progressively advance to full effectiveness and to guarantee that these rights will be exercised without any type of discrimination.

It is worth reminding ourselves that among the rights contained in the Covenant is the right to work, which includes the opportunity to earn one's living at work that is freely chosen or accepted. If the states are to make this right fully effective, they must adopt measures to provide technical and professional training along with laws and ways to achieve development with full employment. This also includes the right to equitable, satisfactory working conditions. It means equal pay for men and women at a wage that permits them to live decently. It means worker health and safety and equal opportunities for promotion and time off. It means the right to form and join unions, and that includes the right to strike.

There is also the right to social security, which includes the right of every person to enjoy the highest possible standard of physical and mental health. The state has an obligation to create conditions that assure that people will receive medical attention and care if they are ill. For women who are mothers, this includes access to proper health care before and after giving birth to a child.

How many of the obligations established in the Covenant are effectively fulfilled by the states? Very few, and what we have seen is often not very solid. What are the existing mechanisms for obliging the states to fulfill their commitments? I believe that one way of ensuring fulfillment would be critical and rigorous examination of the reports governments submit to the Committee responsible for overseeing fulfillment of the Covenant. This examination should be carried out by international organizations and their evaluations should be widely circulated, showing both the achievements and the difficulties encountered along the way. Governments are sensitive to having this type of information made public and at the present time neither the reports nor their evaluations are widely circulated.

Nevertheless, some things appear to be changing. The twentieth century has left us heirs to various paradoxes in the area of law. On one hand, the concept of justice as an ethical ideal has now spread across geographic and political boundaries. It has begun to break down some cultural barriers and is beginning to link peoples who are proposing to consolidate the principles of equity, respect and dignity for all human beings. On the other hand, this desire for justice appears to be contrary to the economic policies designed by the international organizations that define the ironclad frameworks for the countries of the world without any care for our needs, ignoring the economic and social rights of millions of people of the Third World.

Structural adjustment programs that diminish the workforce and limit access to health and education through privatization are presented as necessary measures for bringing our people out of poverty and backwardness. Countries that resist are ostracized and their people must suffer inhuman economic sanctions and restrictions.

How do we bring abut the right to a decent life, to health, to work, to education, when nearly one-third of all our financial resources must be spent on servicing the international debt and when our role in the international division of labor is to produce cheap labor and buy everything on credit from the developed countries—from technology to cheap gadgets and toys? What place is there for protective laws and for the international commitments states have made—such as the Beijing Platform for Action and other agreements aimed at progressively improving the living conditions and the social, economic and cultural rights of the peoples—in a climate of market flexibilization?

## Economic Discrimination and Inequality

The Convention on the Elimination of All Forms of Discrimination against Women (CEDAW) specifically refers to the economic, social and cultural rights of women, signaling that "discrimination...shall mean any distinction, exclusion or restriction on the basis of sex which has the effect or purpose of impairing or nullifying the recognition, enjoyment or exercise by women, irrespective of their marital status, on a basis of equality of men and women, of human rights and fundamental freedoms in the political, economic, social, cultural, civil or any other field." In other words, women's economic, social and cultural rights are the same as men's and they are applicable to all in all their diversity.

The world conferences at Vienna, Copenhagen, and Beijing served to promote further directions for the indivisibility, interdependence and interconnectedness of human rights, but they did not establish mechanisms to guarantee development and policy change or commitments to combat poverty.

To use the case of Colombia as an example, in addition to incorporating the international human rights instruments into national legislation, in recent years some progress had been made towards designing national development plans that incorporate gender equity. This process was assisted by the new Constitution adopted in 1991, which includes respect for human rights as one of its fundamental pillars, and which specifically states that women and men have equal rights. However, in the last two years we have seen a retreat from policies that focus on gender equity and address the human rights and development needs of women. In Colombia, the National Office for Women's Equity, which was established during the previous administration, has been closed and replaced by a council that has no institutional structure to link it to the different branches of government.

This turning back from measures to guarantee women's human rights reflects the dangerous effects of structural adjustment policies on the region, which impose economic globalization according to the dictates of the developed countries. The poor, who lack education and access to technology, are the first to be affected. And the poorest of the poor are women, who were excluded from these benefits long before structural adjustment was introduced.

The question we should be asking is: "Does the social reality correspond to national and international legislative advances and the few institutional advances that have been achieved? Has the situation of Latin American women improved?"

We cannot say that the answer is positive. Our countries, which have been required to submit to economic adjustment processes in order to adapt to the economic reality of globalization, have taken measures that impact negatively on the poorest and most vulnerable groups, and women have suffered the worst consequences. This should not come as a surprise to us, given the history of exclusion that we know so well. If women have always been the most unprotected members of society, any restrictive or limiting measure will affect them severely. Studies in the region have shown that the effects of structural adjustment policies fall heavily on women, who are forced to enter the labor market under unfavorable conditions. The negative effects of globalization—the inequitable distribution of benefits, unemployment, the shutting down of social security institutions, the loss of cultural identity, fewer public schools, and unequal access to the new information and communication technologies—simply accentuate the traditional gender inequalities.

Governments may make good-sounding speeches but they don't do very much, especially when it comes to women. When there are cutbacks to economic policies, women are the ones who feel the strongest impact. And it is precisely that which I think we are going to be seeing during this Beijing + 5 process. I think we are going to see that progress hasn't been that great because governments are largely made up of men and frankly, they are not that interested. When we reach a point where there are women in decision-making positions and when we finally see a lot of women in national, local, and regional congresses, I think then we will be able to see clear advances in the interconnectedness, indivisibility, and universality of women's human rights.

## The Challenges of Globalization

The dependent situation of the countries of Latin America, their precarious technological development, the scarcity of economic resources without reasonable investment priorities, the institutional weakness and strongly male dominated cultural traditions are formidable obstacles for putting in place a culture of respect for the economic, social and cultural rights of women. If we add to these disadvantages the negative effects of economic globalization, the weaknesses are accentuated and new ones are created.

I believe that the first big challenge for Latin America is the consolidation of political democracy. Our governments are being squeezed between the dictates of the great powers that insist on transforming economies to fit economic globalization and the social demands of the growing mass of the population that is becoming poorer every day. They can't satisfy either, and this generates instability and is a serious danger to the survival of democracy. There are many examples of how this is being played out.

Political stability is indispensable for economic development. Latin America should define how far it is willing to go in making concessions to globalization and what it intends to do to attend to the social demands of a population that cannot satisfy its basic needs on its own. It has been pointed out by some analysts that many of the social benefits that support human development are provided through non-market means and run the risk of being eliminated by the rules of competition. Governments must become better organized if they are to take advantage of global markets and foster competitiveness, so that we can achieve globalization with ethics and equity—a globalization that includes everybody and where development is synonymous with human security and sustainability. In other words, a globalization that works for people, not just for profit, and that ensures that there are adequate human, community and environmental resources to achieve these goals. We must continue to ask ourselves: Why is it that the laws of the market can be globalized, but not the demand to make human rights effective through agreements that were supposedly freely established? How do we achieve a globalization that incorporates ethics and equity, that is inclusive, and that is characterized by human security, sustainability and development?

The second challenge lies in achieving regional integration in order to overcome the weakness of our relationship with the rest of the world. Now that political polarization has ceased to exist, the great powers have set up areas of economic influence that have immense power to manipulate dependent economies.

Our region has remained behind when it comes to combining our particular strengths in order to confront the powerful countries, which are only interested in profit, economic efficiency and capital flow. Integration will permit our countries to develop their economies and regional and international trade more efficiently while, at the same time, influencing the new balance of power in the areas of peace and security, defense of the environment and the transfer of new technologies. Regional integration will permit Latin America to take stock of its natural resources and create legal and cultural barriers so that the genetic properties of the biological species will not be put to the exclusive service of capital and so that all of humanity may benefit from them. These legal barriers would prevent the unilateral flow of ideas, knowledge and creativity of the rich countries to the poor ones, along with the risk this implies in terms of the loss of cultural identity. But regional integration will not be possible without the support of the United Nations and the Organization of American States (OAS), whose role as mediators between rich and poor nations can reduce the impact of regulations that are not sensitive to the existing inequalities in wealth distribution.

### Women's Role in Constructing Justice

It should be emphasized that women are fighting for full human rights and the realization of the ideals of freedom, equality, and solidarity, not just for women, but for all people. The struggle is about human rights for all, without discrimination. Every person—every man and woman whose cultural, social economic, or political rights have been violated—has found allies in the feminist struggle. From this point of view, the construction of justice is not a question of sex. The focus of feminism has moved to a place where the process of realizing full human rights is not about women versus men but about excluded citizens versus cultural patterns, practices and social stereotypes that give rise to discrimination. This is a struggle against discriminatory social practices.

To reduce the women's movement to a struggle for women's rights only is to diminish its credibility, since women are not the only ones who's right to work, health, social security, education and development go unrecognized. Acceptance of a limited concept of the women's movement is contradictory to the ideals of equality and to the universality and interdependence of human rights. Human rights are for all and cannot be limited to specific sectors.

In this new order, it is not only necessary to strengthen women's organizations and promote the forming of women's networks. We must advance to collective actions with other social organizations that are pursuing the same rights from wherever they are positioned. This is what the branch of the women's movement that is fighting for a radical and plural democracy, that will guarantee the full exercise of citizenship, is trying to do. Radical democracy means that you cannot have democracy while maintaining the current structures of oppression, exclusion and exploitation. The role of women, therefore, is not only to struggle against the dominant social order of capitalism and patriarchy, but also against new and old exploitative modes of production. At the same time, women have and will continue to play a fundamental role in the struggle to overcome the kind of treatment in the public and private spheres that has served as a basis for the survival of a great deal of discrimination. The untouchable nature of the private sphere has impeded the possibility of decisive actions for eradicating such aberrant practices as domestic violence, the unfair sexual division of domestic labor and sexual attacks against women and girls.

To sum up, the role of women is universal. Fighting for respect for human rights means being on the side of the excluded and marginalized. I believe that women's role in conceiving justice as an ethical principle has been molded through practice for over two centuries. This commitment to building justice is not a question of which sex one is. It is about achieving fully implemented human rights. It is an essential commitment, not only of and for women, but for all of humanity, and this is the way we have always understood it. And that solidarity represents such a formidable strength in the face of market domination that it fills us with hope that we will eventually achieve a more just social order.

# Notes

1. The Universal Declaration of Human Rights (UDHR) is the basic international pronouncement of the fundamental rights of all human beings. The Universal Declaration was proclaimed by the United Nations on December 10, 1948 as the "common standard of achievement for all peoples and all nations." It outlines the inalienable rights for all humanity and has set the direction for all further work in the area of human rights.

2. The International Covenant on Economic, Social and Cultural Rights is one of the six core treaties of the international human rights system. It was adopted by the UN General Assembly in 1966 and entered into force in 1976.

3. The Convention on the Elimination of All Forms of Discrimination against Women (CEDAW) is sometimes referred to as the Women's Convention. It was adopted by the United Nations in 1979 and entered into force on September 3, 1981.

# We Want it Paid With Interest!

Asma Jahangir

It is important to remember that governments have a legal commitment to respect the Beijing process. Their failure at this Beijing + 5 Review to stay with that commitment, or to try and hedge on it, would really be a violation of that international commitment. It is that message that we need to bring to the proceedings this week. It is also important for us to emphasize that women's rights have advanced—that we have already gone beyond Beijing—and indeed even before Beijing, the rights of women actually attained progress, often in spite of governments. It is women themselves who have been able to help, have been able to devise strategies, have in fact brought progress for women around the world.

It is also notable that women today are leaders in many ways. Women are leaders in civil society, not just at the international level or the regional level, but much more so at the local level, where they have been innovative, where they have met each other, where they have used communication skills which have actually been able to draw more and more people—not just women—to address the questions of violations of rights.

Women in Pakistan have often been asked, "How is it that women are more organized? How is it that the seminars that women organize are far better than the ones that are mixed or just organized by men?" And the answer is

*Asma Jahangir is the United Nations Special Rapporteur on Extrajudicial, Summary and Arbitrary Executions.*

simply because women are more committed. Women are not just advocates of the rights of women—we are also the sufferers. For us it is not just an academic question. It is very much a question of our survival, and for many women, one of basic survival.

Women have given special expertise in this regard, and we have been able to organize ourselves differently. We have been able to devise capacities which communicate not just to women, but to other people as well. There has been a different kind of discourse—a discourse which is frank, which is open, which is clear. The women's movement has not been an inward-looking movement.

## A Critical Social Movement

The women's movement today is the critical movement in all social movements, because it does not just change the plight of women. It changes everything in society. It not only changes the status of women, but the status of children and of men, the status of other vulnerable groups, the status of minority women within a minority group. When we talk of double jeopardy, we have to ensure that the movement takes with us women that belong to minority majority groups as well as those that belong to minority groups within our own communities.

This movement must bring a reallocation of resources. It will go ahead and forge the agenda for peace. It challenges militarization; it challenges the arms race. No wonder the Beijing process is a challenge for governments. It means an end to the old status quo. Today, while we ask for our rights from governments, we are in a position to actually ask for an apology because these are rights that should have been given to us yesterday and are being denied to us even today.

We are talking about mainstreaming, and I find it extremely important that women's issues are not only mainstreamed at the national, regional, and international levels, but that women themselves also mainstream their work with other mechanisms at both the national and international levels. I have seen that when that does take place, it has a powerful effect.

## Women Working for Peace

I would like to share with you a few of my experiences as a Special Rapporteur in the UN system. I saw remarkable incidents of courage and those incidents of courage by women are never, ever documented. For example, in the conflict in Kosovo, I met refugee women who were coming across to Skopje, and many of them told me stories of how they saved the lives of men. And what was so remarkable was when one of us asked them, "Who was this man? Was he a Serb or a Kosovo Albanian?" And they said, "I didn't ask, but his life was in danger." And this is only possible where there are women who live ordinary lives, who have ordinary thoughts and a remarkable sense of commitment and courage.

I met women in East Timor, and there was a woman whose husband was with the Indonesian army and he had defected and was hiding in West Timor. She gave testimony: "I know that my husband can be in danger for giving this testimony. But I think it is important for the world to know that the militia was patronized by the army." And after she gave her testimony, I said to her, "Why do you think it's important to know that the militia was patronized by the army?" She said, "It's important to know, because this is a new game of all the armies around the world. And I don't want a repetition of it, so I have to speak up."

Similarly, we have testimonies of other women—women who were vulnerable, women who have suffered. But they did not come to give testimony because they felt that it would glorify them. They came to testify because they wanted an end to violence, and not just an end to violence in East Timor, but an end to violence the world over.

We have seen, for example, problems that women face which are not being addressed. In Nepal, we saw a number of women who were in the Maoist insurgent movement. And some of them felt that life had nothing else to offer them, so possibly a militant revolutionary movement could give them a better life. And there were some who said, "We left home, but it is now never possible for us to go back. And therefore for us, it is a life of complete militancy and to remain in this movement."

There are hundreds of stories that we have all come across. We have seen women engaging in diplomacy. We saw recently in Pakistan and India, when tensions were high, thirty women from India drove to Pakistan in the midst of hostilities and threats, and they came with a message of peace. They did not speak about differences, but they spoke about commonalities. They did not speak about aggression, but they spoke about peace and living together, understanding each other. And I remember the words of the leader of the delegation, who said, "I teach sometimes, and I tell the students 'gone are the days when you can call yourself a citizen of India. You are first a citizen of the world.'" And it is with that message that she came.

Similarly, it was not "possible" for any Pakistani to return that visit, but sixty-four women went from Pakistan with the message of peace. And it was through their discourse, a discourse at the level of culture, where they were able to sing to each other, where they were able to give the same kind of stories to each other that we learned as children, that brought the whole thing to an emotional level, and yet we were able to discuss all the difficult problems between us. We were not shying away from it. And I think that that turned out to be possibly the best people-to-people diplomacy that has been tried between India and Pakistan for many years. And the reason was because we believed, as women, in peace.

## Standing Up To Government Resistance

As a Special Rapporteur, I have wondered when a woman's right to movement has been denied by the government and she goes forth anyway, despite government restriction, would her life not be threatened? If she is killed, would that not be an extra-judicial killing? If a woman refuses to abide by the dress code that has been applied to her by the government, and if she is lynched by non-state actors at the behest of the government, would that not be an extra-judicial killing? There are many women in this world who live under such threats and who live with people's contempt.

One of the strategies that I would like to see is that women's groups target the worst countries in terms of their treatment of women. And I do not say societies, because countries—through their borders—are countries. A society across the border may have different kinds of norms for women. We have to look at the worst country, where women cannot breathe, where women cannot smile, where women cannot walk out, where women cannot talk freely, where women cannot wear what they want, cannot think what they want—and these are the countries that we need to target and isolate their governments.

When we talk about strategies at the national level, we need to look at the laws. We also need to look at traditional practices which women have to defy. The High Commissioner was very much right in saying that we all respect culture and religion, and I often say that, as women, we are far more religious and far closer to culture than men are. But we cannot, in the name of religion and culture, accept to be violated. And I have seen that often enough in our own country of Pakistan. Only the day before yesterday there was a statement by our ambassador saying, "Yes, we respect CEDAW,[1] but only subject to Islamic norms."

And what are the Islamic norms? The ambassador doesn't know. What are the Islamic norms? The government doesn't know. So the government should, perhaps, have sent a few Islamic clergy here, provided they would agree among themselves as to what Islamic norms are, to tell us exactly what it is in CEDAW that they do not respect?

We have seen this politicization of culture and politicization of religion. We are women who represent all religions and all cultures here. Our rights take priority over all. Therefore, we have to help each other in actually overcoming man-made customs that humiliate us. We have to look at the rights of minority women. We have to get women into decision-making power. We have to mobilize women at the grassroots. We must have access, especially in the Third World, to electronic media, because education otherwise is not possible. We have to give input into the political directions of our countries. A theocratic country, a militarized country, cannot give rights to anybody, including women.

At the regional level, we have to forge partnerships where we can focus on peace. Cross-country tensions and terrorism of non-state actors give rise to fundamentalism, and consequently the rights of women are violated. At the United Nations level, we have to mainstream gender issues. To my mind, it is not done often. But then, the input also has to come from the women's movement.

And to end, I think that whatever the governments are going to be doing in the next few days, let us be quite clear that that is a debt they owe to us—a debt that they should have paid to us centuries ago. We want it paid with interest and we do not want a restructuring to our disadvantage. Thank you.

## Note

1. CEDAW is the abbreviation commonly used to refer to the Convention on the Elimination of All Forms of Discrimination against Women, sometimes called the Women's Convention. The Convention entered into force on September 3, 1981.

# The Achievements and Challenges of the Women's Human Rights Movement

*Florence Butegwa*

WOMEN FROM AROUND THE WORLD HAVE CAUSE TO CELEBRATE the last ten years. For in this period, we who are gathered here, and the millions who are not here, have taken our place in history. We have built upon the various struggles of the women who were activists before us—in the suffrage and civil rights movements, in the independence movements, in the labor movements, and in the health movements. We have learned from and built upon the work of those who advocated for a more equitable place for women in the development process, in education, in religion and in politics. We have learned and built upon the inner strengths and resistance of millions of women who suffered gender-based violence in their personal lives and in public spaces. We have learned from women in the Global South, wherever it may be geographically located, for whom extreme poverty has meant the denial of any opportunity to devote their energies to breaking the yoke of gender-based subordination and discrimination. We have to celebrate because over the last ten years, we have taken these struggles and repositioned them at the centers of power at the national, regional and international levels. By placing women's concerns and aspirations within a human rights paradigm, we have made a powerful and undeniable proposition: That women are human and that on that basis, they claim and are entitled to the fundamental rights and freedoms inherent in all humanity.

*Florence Butegwa is a Ugandan human rights lawyer and feminist activist.*

## There Have Been Many Achievements

This conceptual breakthrough and organizing framework is perhaps one of the major achievements of the movement, for it enables us to work together as women without the need to gloss over our diversity or look at it as a weakness. For each woman—rich or poor; white or black or whatever color might be used to describe an entire race; heterosexual, lesbian or bisexual; educated or not; minority; or physically challenged—each one of us is entitled to fundamental human rights. We are able to make demands as women and yet allow the diversity within us to define what equality or freedom of speech or bodily integrity—or other rights—mean for us in our circumstances or the various ways in which these rights are violated. This is what I see as the basis of a global women's human rights movement, allowing each one of us the space and the support to undertake political advocacy on both our individual issues *and* those of other women, even where we perceive them as different. Positioning our demands for equality and femaleness unfettered by socially constructed and stereotypical obstacles has given women incredible access and opened up new sites for political work. Women can now justifiably demand the right to be heard at sessions of any United Nations body, at the World Bank and the International Monetary Fund and at the state and local government levels. We can justifiably demand the right, not only to be heard, but also to be visible and to be our own interlocutors.

Through collective advocacy and theoretical work, the women's human rights movement can today celebrate quite a number of other achievements. First, the movement has played a key role in the development of human rights standards at the international, regional and national levels. Examples at the United Nations level include the recent adoption of the Optional Protocol to CEDAW,[1] and the Declaration on the Elimination of Violence Against Women in 1993,[2] as well as the ongoing work on trafficking in persons. The movement has also been active within the regional human rights systems and new standards relating to women are emerging. Examples include the Convention on the Prevention, Punishment and Eradication of Violence against Women of the Inter-American System for the Protection of Human Rights,[3] and the proposed Additional Protocol on Women's Human Rights under the African Charter on Human and Peoples' Rights.[4] At the national level, activists have successfully influenced parliaments to expand constitutional and other legislative guarantees to include women's human rights.

Feminist activists and academics have been instrumental in promoting the reinterpretation of existing standards so as to include women's experiences. The movement has played a leading role in the conceptualization of human rights in a manner that either eliminates or narrows the dichotomy between the public and the private sphere. This is particularly true of our work on violence against women and reproductive and sexuality rights. By asserting that the state is obligated to ensure that women's human rights are respected in the family and community, we have shattered the notion of a private domain which is outside the purview of human rights and the state. We have also re-energized claims for the indivisibility of human rights. Within the academic institutions, we must celebrate the fact that women's human rights is a discipline that is now taught in many universities and colleges. The partnership between feminists in academia and the activists has been one of our major strengths.

We can celebrate our role in strengthening institutional frameworks for the promotion and protection of women's human rights. At the United Nations level, many of us are familiar with the Special Rapporteur on Violence Against Women, Its Causes and Consequences. We celebrate the establishment of the Special Rapporteur and the tremendous work that she has been able to do. She would not have been able to accomplish so much without the support of the entire movement. In the same vein, when we define our achievements, we must include all the various ways in which we have contributed to the growth of other human rights organs through our participation and demands. The Committee on the Elimination of Discrimination Against Women, the Human Rights Commission in Geneva, and its Sub-Commission have a better perception, at least, of the fact that women's human rights must remain a constant in their work and that this fact calls for substantive and procedural changes. There are women's human rights focal points and programs in the secretariats of the various UN Commissions and specialized bodies.

Women's human rights activists have developed tools for strengthening our work. While some of us initially depended on intuition, now there are training models and handbooks, leadership institutes, networking models, academic theory and documentation of our work. These are tools which we, and future generations, can refer to and learn from in order to do better organizing. We can, hopefully, avoid repeating some of the anxieties, mistakes or weaknesses of the past. This also implies a big responsibility for all of us to document and develop tools as we go along, so that we contribute to developing capacity and avoid women reinventing the wheel instead of devoting their energies and resources to the substantive work.

The movement can also celebrate the development of leadership in the area of women's human rights work at the international, regional, and national levels through sharing our leadership, through training and mentoring, and through the creation of opportunities and spaces for others to participate and learn. In addition, many women have made constructive inputs for various leadership models to grow and the movement is that much richer in terms of leadership resources.

## Challenges

As any student of political science or sociology will know, progress comes with new challenges. The progress that women have made in asserting their rights and demanding accountability is worrying conservative and anti-feminist forces at the national and international levels. These groups are organized, and unfortunately, well funded. Many have appropriated human rights language and are a visible force at United Nations gatherings and in other corridors of power. They are determined to use all means at their disposal to reverse the gains that women have made. How we organize against or in spite of these reactionary forces is a major challenge to the movement. Do we have the resources? Do we have the analytical finesse to identify the negative messages in what is positioned as human rights parlance? Do we have the networks to alert each other and to have quick, coordinated reactions before damage is done?

In addition, there are challenges that we, and future generations of activists, must face. For convenience, I will group them into three categories: conceptual, methodological and organizational.

## Conceptual Clarity

As we take our work to new heights, we need to refine and clarify the theory that underpins it. This needs to go beyond the academic realm, so that there is consistency. Time does not permit me to go into detail, but let me pose some questions: Are demands for women's human rights based on notions of equality with, or difference from, men? In our work on violence against women, and in the areas of reproductive and sexuality rights, is our demand for the recognition of new rights, or the reinterpretation of existing rights? Are specific rights implicated in different forms of violence against women? Or are we demanding that states recognize a generic, fundamental freedom from gender-based violence?

Another challenge arises from the advances we have made in holding states accountable for violations by non-state actors. How do we consolidate the jurisprudence on this point, and its acceptance in international and national law? How many of us have instituted cases seeking to hold our governments accountable for the widespread violence that women suffer at the hands of male partners or strangers? On this point, is this an opportune time to take a leaf from the Rome Statute of the International Criminal Court[5] and call for individual accountability for violations of women's human rights?

## Methodological Challenges

I want to raise four methodological challenges. The first arises from our demands for the mainstreaming of gender and women's human rights. *How does one mainstream women's human rights?* We can no longer rely on the rhetoric. We have been heard. There is a UN resolution calling for mainstreaming in the work of all human rights bodies. Are we ready to provide the necessary leadership with concrete recommendations about what each human rights body needs to do? A subsidiary, but important question that is rarely asked is whether calls for mainstreaming gender imply a need for us to mainstream our work? The second methodological challenge focuses on documentation and analysis of women's experiences from a human rights perspective. One of the demands that we often make is that UN human rights mechanisms and so-called human rights NGOs solicit information from women's organizations at the national level so that investigations reflect women's experiences. To what extent are we developing the capacity to make the necessary information available in an accessible format? More important: To what extent are we developing the capacity so that documentation and analysis is a continuing process and so that the information supports women's human rights advocacy at the national and local levels? Such specific information is necessary for developing appropriate legal and other standards and for redress for women whose rights are violated. The documentation must be linked to making women's human rights real to women on a day-to-day basis.

## Organizational Challenges

Since the World Conference on Human Rights in 1993,[6] more and more women and their organizations identify themselves with the women's human rights movement. They have provided very valuable inputs into the Cairo, Copenhagen, and Beijing processes. Many have continued to work at the national level—bringing the outcomes of these processes home and holding states accountable. We do not want to lose this momentum. We do not want to lose the gains that have been made over the last decades. Those of you who have been involved in advocacy in sessions of the various UN human rights bodies, including the Commission on the Status of Women and the Human Rights Commission, will know that conservative forces are mobilized to prevent further advances for women's human rights and to restrict even the achievements that have been made. Unfortunately, most of us—particularly from developing countries—are not regular in maintaining a presence at these sessions and monitoring state actions. The reasons that prevent our presence are many. The question is: How do we prevent the loss of gains that have been made? How do we make optimum use of the resources of the movement to maintain a presence at the various UN and regional processes? How can we have input even if we are unable to be physically present?

The challenges are not meant to take away from the validity of our celebration of the achievements, for they are many. They are, in fact, evidence of progress and of our connection with a changing world. The challenges, and women's determination to face them, are evidence of women's claim to full citizenship in the world—whatever way it is configured. Ladies and Gentlemen, I thank you.

# Notes

1. CEDAW is the abbreviation commonly used to refer to the Convention on the Elimination of All forms of Discrimination against Women, sometimes called the Women's Convention. CEDAW entered into force on September 3, 1981. The Optional Protocol to CEDAW is an additional formal instrument, separate from the CEDAW convention, that introduces a procedure whereby the Committee on the Elimination of Discrimination Against Women (called the CEDAW Committee) can receive and investigate complaints of cases of discrimination against women, including those brought forth by individuals, in countries that have ratified both CEDAW and the Optional Protocol. At the time of this writing, there is a growing campaign to convince a greater number of member states to adopt the Optional Protocol.

2. The Declaration on the Elimination of Violence Against Women was adopted by the UN General Assembly on December 20, 1993. While it does not have the legal force of an international treaty or convention, the Declaration is useful as a tool in interpreting international treaties. It also serves as a standard setting device, indicating the international community's position on the subject of violence against women.

3. The Convention on the Prevention, Punishment and Eradication of Violence against Women entered into force on March 5, 1995. It is often referred to as the Convention of Belem do Pará after the city in Brazil where it was adopted by the General Assembly of the Organization of American States (OAS). The Convention is the first and only multilateral human rights treaty that focuses exclusively on violence against women. The Inter-American System for the Promotion and Protection of Human Rights is the regional human rights system of the OAS.

4. The African Charter on Human and Peoples' Rights is also known as the Banjul Charter on Human and Peoples' Rights. Its text was approved at Banjul, Gambia in January 1981. Women's

organizations have pointed out that women's rights are inadequately covered in the Charter. They have responded to this vacuum by drafting the Additional Protocol on Women's Rights, which explicitly states that women's rights as human rights must be respected and observed.

5. The Rome Statute is the treaty document that provides the legal basis for creation of an International Criminal Court (ICC). It was finalized in July 1998 following several years of negotiations. The ICC is a permanent judicial body, which the UN is in the process of creating, with a mandate to investigate and punish genocide, crimes against humanity and war crimes in circumstances in which national authorities fail to do so. The Rome Statute contains many provisions for the prosecution of wartime violence against women, codifying various acts constituting sexual and gender violence as the most serious crimes under international humanitarian law. It is empowered to determine individual criminal responsibility where appropriate. (See Barbara Bedont and Katherine Hall-Martinez, "Ending Impunity for Gender Crimes under the International Criminal Court," *The Brown Journal of World Affairs*, VI:1 (1999): 65-85. Also available at http://www.crlp.org/icc.html.) For more information about the ICC, see: http://www.un.org/law/icc.

6. Largely due to the organizing work of women around the world, the World Conference on Human Rights, which took place in Vienna in 1993, marks the first time that women's rights were recognized as human rights. The Vienna Declaration and Programme of Action states that "gender-based violence and all forms of sexual harassment and exploitation, including those resulting from cultural prejudice and international trafficking, are incompatible with the dignity and worth of the human person, and must be eliminated."

## Let's Light Another Candle
*for the fourteen women, and the fourteen x fourteen millions more*

...Let's light a candle

Let's light another candle
For old women, rejected wives, and all women
 Powerless and silenced,
Whose children have forgotten the ones who gave them birth
Let's light a candle,

Let's light another candle,
For childless wives, violated women and all women scorned
Whose brothers have forgotten the same mothers they mourned
Let's light a candle,

Let's light another candle
For women mutilated by parents, battered by
 partners,
 All women killed by laws of custom,
Whose families hold sacrosanct such "cultural
 practice",
Let's light a candle,

Let's light another candle
For "comfort women," "ethnically polluted"
 women,
 All women brutalized by rape and the
 sanctions of war
Whose states have abandoned them;
 displaced, seeking refuge
Let's light a candle,

Let's light another candle
For girl children unmourned in death,
 oppressed in life,
 All girls unborn to life,
Whose people place no honour in girls
Let's light a candle,

Let's light another candle
Also for warrior women working for women,
All females, all feminists, all sisters in spirit,
Let's light a candle.

Let's light another candle.

*Abena P.A. Busia is on the faculty of the Departments of English and Women's Studies at Rutgers University. Her poetry has been published widely around the world.*

*This poem celebrates the 16 Days of Activism Against Gender Violence. It was first read in 1995 at a memorial service organized by the Canadian High Commission in Accra, Ghana, to commemorate the fourteen women who died in the Montreal Massacre in 1989.*

*©Abena P.A. Busia, Accra, December 6, 1995. Reprinted by permission of author.*

*Part II:*
*Innovative Praxis*

## Section 1

## Violence Against Women: New Strategies for Confronting Discrimination and Abuse

VIOLENCE AGAINST WOMEN IS THE CLEAREST, MOST PERVASIVE manifestation of the inequality women experience in societies throughout the world. It is also an issue that women's persistent efforts have succeeded in making visible. As a result of women's organizing, violence against women was first recognized as a human rights issue at the World Conference on Human Rights in Vienna in 1993. Only two years later, in the Beijing Platform for Action, states agreed to work to put an end to gender-based violence, and this commitment was reiterated during the Beijing + 5 Review. However, they refused to accept a proposal for formal international collaboration to collect data on violence against women, because they did not want to be subject to international monitoring in this area. Without real statistics on the incidence of gender violence in the world today, it will be hard to take concrete measures to end it.

The testimonies that follow provide examples of some of the types of violence women are experiencing and what they are doing to confront it. They illustrate the way in which private behavior and state action or complicity with violence are interwoven. They also tell us something about the vigor and creativity women are bringing to the struggle against gender-based violence.

Increasingly, women's organizations are developing the capacity to research, document and publicize cases of human rights abuse and the ability to utilize communications media for shaping public opinion. In some cases, this is being achieved with the help of journalists who have been sensitized to women's human rights issues. This type of collaboration is perhaps best illustrated in the example provided by Ivonne Macassi of Peru, in which several organizations collaborated to identify and document abuses and to prepare a report that could be used to build a case against the government health care system. Allies working in the media aided the process by publishing advance coverage of the report and by providing the researchers with tips about other cases of abuse they had learned about. In this situation, the women's organizations were successful in bringing about policy changes that will make it easier for the public to bring complaints against the health care system in the future. Unfortunately, the case also highlights the difficulty groups that receive government funding may have in speaking out about government wrongdoing. This situation has resonance for groups in a similar position everywhere.

The example of the Medica Zenica group in Bosnia-Herzegovina focuses on the sexual and physical violence women experienced during the recent armed conflict in that region, and which continues to take place after the war has stopped. The case presented by Duška Andric-Ruzicic raises the issue of governments using public outrage about women's pain and abuse for their own political ends. It also offers frank observations on the difficulties that can arise when grassroots women's organizations become the experts in an area and begin to provide training for professionals in the legal, medical or law enforcement fields who may then feel that their competence is being challenged.

While the story presented by Elizabeth Khaxas of Sister Namibia did not include documented cases of physical violence, lesbians became the target of insults and threatening remarks from members of the government while, in practice, their human rights were being violated on a number of fronts. The targeting of women's sexuality became the pretext for disqualifying a progressive political document that had been drafted by a diverse group of women, as well as some men, with the goal of seeking equality for women in society. Sister Namibia's success in combating homophobic and discriminatory government policy is a credit to women's solidarity and organizing, and to the respect the group has earned in Namibian society.

In one of the most difficult cases presented in this book, Nadera Shalhoub-Kevorkian describes the work her organization is doing to save the lives of women under threat of death from their families for supposed transgressions of "honor." In redefining this act of woman killing as "femicide," she moves beyond discussion of tradition or honor in connection with the killings. The human rights abuses she describes are being carried out against a background of war, displacement and political uncertainty, while the women under threat are often victims of multiple abuses, including rape and incest. Using strategies that combine modern technology and psychological counseling, Shalhoub-Kevorkian and her team are attempting to save women's lives while trying to change the way women are viewed in the family and in society.

Indai Sajor shows us how violations of women's human rights during World War II are linked to abuses taking place today. The Tokyo Tribunal has served to bring sexual violence and armed conflict into focus while seeking redress for women who were forced into sexual slavery by the Japanese Army over fifty years ago. The Tribunal, which has received international attention, attests to the tenacity of the women who were unwilling to let past abuses go unrecognized and unpunished. It provides an example of international collaboration among women.

The cases that follow are but five examples of the types of abuses women are experiencing around the world. In the context of the Beijing + 5 Review, they can serve to remind us of the tremendous amount of work that still needs to be done if the promise of Beijing is to be fulfilled. In the meantime, women, as usual, are busy filling the gap between promise and reality.

# Silence and Complicity: Unmasking Abuses of Women's Human Rights in the Peruvian Health Care System

Ivonne Macassi

*Ivonne Macassi is Executive Director of the Peruvian women's organization, Flora Tristán. She was one of the researchers who worked on the report "Silence and Complicity," which exposed human rights abuses in the Peruvian public health system.*

*El Centro de la Mujer Peruana "Flora Tristán" was founded in 1979 by a group of women who wanted to build a feminist institution that would make the real situation of women visible and defend women's rights. Over the years, the group has become a reference point for women's organizations in Peru and other Latin American countries and for Peruvian society in general with regard to women's issues.*

I AM SPEAKING FROM THE PERSPECTIVE OF MY ORGANIZATION, the Peruvian women's group, Centro de la Mujer Peruana "Flora Tristán." The experience I am going to talk about took place during 1996 and 1997. I am going to focus on the events leading up to a report our group prepared on violations of women's human rights by people working in the Peruvian public health system. These include documented cases involving gender based violence, violations of the right to health and violations of sexual and reproductive rights. The study on which the report was based was carried out through an agreement between Flora Tristán, the Latin American and Caribbean Committee for the Defense of Human Rights (CLADEM), and the New York-based Center for Law and Reproductive Policy (CRLP).

Peru is a heterogeneous, pluricultural, multiethnic country in which several languages are in common use. It has a population of approximately 26 million people, 28 percent of which live in rural areas. About 50 percent of the population is poor and 80 percent of the poor are rural dwellers. Peruvian institutions are in a very fragile state. The current government is characterized by centralization and authoritarianism, both of which make it difficult for people, especially women, to exercise their rights.

## Reports of Abuse

During 1994 and 1995, Flora Tristán began receiving repeated complaints of practices by service providers in the public health hospitals that are in violation of women's human rights. We received complaints about acts of physical and psychological violence and cases in which women's lives, bodies, and general health were exposed to grave risks. We also heard about cases of coercive, humiliating and discriminatory treatment against women during childbirth or who arrived at the hospitals for treatment and were subsequently accused of having had an abortion.[1] This motivated us to carry out an investigation in order to uncover the magnitude of the problem so that we could both reveal the causes and seek ways of correcting the situation.

We decided to produce a report based on documented cases in order to show clear evidence of the human rights violations that were taking place. I am not going to go into detail about the methodology we used for carrying out the study. Basically, what we did was present a sample of cases that took place in the three very different geographic/social zones of our country—the coast, the mountains and the jungle. We interviewed individuals and groups, both users of the public health system and service providers, including doctors, nurses and obstetricians. To do this, we carried out a survey with a random sample of women who are users of the public health system. We also carried out field visits to each of the three regions in order to verify information contained in the findings. Finally, we held in-depth interviews with both victims and agents of the health system. Some of the things we learned are the following:

There was a higher incidence of violence and discrimination against women who are young, women living in poverty, rural women, and women living in poor urban neighborhoods. In the relationship between health care users and providers, we found that the providers often presented an attitude that was disapproving, punishing or controlling with regard to women's sexuality and reproductive decisions. Many health workers displayed a paternalistic attitude and there were also extreme cases involving coercion, deception, false information and violence. There was no system whereby health services users could initiate or follow through on actions against administrative authorities or judges who abused their power.

Although it had not been the original purpose of the investigation to monitor the way in which the National Family Planning and Reproductive Health Program was being carried out, we found clear evidence of cases in which women were not acting with informed consent as well as specific cases of abuse in the area of "voluntary surgical contraception," or sterilization. The following are some examples of cases from among the seventy we documented during our investigation.

Marina, a twenty-three-year-old woman, went to the emergency ward of the hospital in the town of Juliata, in Puno province, complaining of a headache and fever. The doctor who saw her carried out a gynecological examination, even though Marina could not see what it had to do with her headache. After taking off her clothes and touching her, he proposed to continue the examination at his private office, claiming that the hospital did not have the instruments he needed to attend to her. He then drove her to his office where he drugged and raped her. This same doctor had already been reported for sexually abusing a fifteen-year-old girl in the same hospital.

Josefa, a woman living in a rural community in the town of Piura in northern Peru, was taken to the hospital by her mother in May 1996 after she lost consciousness from hemorrhaging. When she regained consciousness the staff accused her of having had an abortion and yelled at her because she had not had her tubes tied. She was left to wait a long time before receiving injections to stop the bleeding. Medical personnel carried out a D and C without any anesthesia and then pressured her to submit to being sterilized.

Zoila, a seventeen-year-old woman, went to the Lima Maternity hospital to give birth to her first child. She told us that she had to wait for over two hours for anyone to see her, in spite of the fact that she was bleeding. When her husband tried to get someone to help her, the nurses told him that they were busy and that she wasn't the only patient.

## Launching an Investigation

These are but three of the testimonies that were collected and verified during the investigation. We quickly designed several strategies based on what we had learned. We set up a system for receiving complaints and the local women's networks made sure women around the country learned how to use it. These local organizations also provided valuable reports which were used in the study and helped us identify and denounce new cases. They also helped to apply pressure locally so that hospitals would have to address the situation. We established direct communication with the investigative units of the main newspapers, and they began to tell us about new cases they learned of. They also provided coverage of the partial findings of our investigation while it was under way.

We developed specific actions for dealing with cases where women were experiencing violence and required immediate intervention. The action plan included presenting documented cases of abuse to the office of the Human Rights Ombudsman and the Women's Commission of the Peruvian Congress. We also took evidence of the cases to the print media, radio, and television. We held a public event where we presented the results of the investigation, making the information available both nationally and internationally. This helped to raise interest in the problem and a number of organizations began to pressure the government to take action.

## Confronting the System

CLADEM took Marina's case to the Inter-American Court of Human Rights. As a result, a so-called "friendly agreement" was reached in which the Peruvian government accepted responsibility for the harm done to her as a user of the public health system. Besides receiving a financial settlement, Marina also received medical treatment and psychological counseling to help her deal with the trauma.

The combined strategies that we used after the report was released led to some important changes in both law and public policy. For one thing, changes have now been made to regulations around the family planning program in Peru, which include some of our recommendations. Among the improvements is an end to demographic targets for family planning, the elimination of mass sterilization campaigns, and the putting in place of a system to guarantee women's informed consent for procedures. The system now requires two counseling sessions for the woman, plus a waiting period of seventy-two hours before giving consent to sterilization. A woman must then sign a form, in the presence of a witness, showing that she gives her permission for the operation to take place.

The government has also begun to develop mechanisms for receiving complaints aimed at the public health establishments so that those responsible for abuse will be identified and sanctioned. Marina's case was a testing ground for the possibility of seeking international protection for human rights cases that affect women, especially where rape is involved.

Finally, I should point out that during the process of preparing the report, we were subject to some unpleasant pressure, especially when we wanted to publish and circulate the results of the investigation. The Peruvian government tried to minimize the impact of the report and some NGOs that work in the area of women's reproductive health participated in this attempt. The government even launched an investigation against our organization in which they tried to discredit us and prevent us from circulating the report. Even some organizations that work with women, that should have been our most important strategic allies, showed ambivalence and fear about going public with this information and were not supportive at all. Thank you.

## Note

1. In Peru, while abortion to save a woman's life is permitted, a woman who is found to have had an abortion for any other reason can be jailed. Peruvian Penal Code, Book II, Title II, Capítulo II, Aborto, Artículo 114.

# Confronting Violence Against Women in the Whole of Society

Duška Andric-Ruzicic

*A former business woman with a background in economics, Duška Andric-Ruzicic coordinates the Infoteka Project of the group Medica Zenica in Bosnia-Herzegovina. Medica Zenica was established in 1993 to offer medical, psychological and practical assistance to women survivors of war violence. Medica has continued to address issues of violence against women in the post-war period. The Infoteka Project carries out research and publication, public advocacy and alternative education with other NGOs and local institutions, while maintaining ongoing networking with local, regional and international activists.*

TWO MONTHS AGO I WAS ASKED TO COOPERATE WITH THE UNITED Nations Development Program by giving my comments on their assessment of the situation in Bosnia-Herzegovina from the development perspective. My task was to concentrate on the gender component, particularly on violence against women. In the original draft, in the section on violence against women, they spoke of two parties—the perpetrator and the victim. This seemed like a betrayal of everything I had learned from my experience, putting violence against women into the private and anonymous sphere. My comments added two additional parts of equal importance—society as a whole, with all its social and non-written rules, social and moral standards and beliefs; and the state, through its institutions ranging from the judicial system, the social support system, the education system, the police and others.

## Using Women's Suffering for Political Goals

I would like to explain why I came to this point of view through my experience of working with women survivors of violence, both as a result of armed conflict and during the so-called peace. After working for seven years in an organization which is mainly dealing with the problem of violence against women, one finds out that the political dimensions of the problem are neglected. There are times when governments want to make the problem of violence against women not that important, and times when they need violence against women as proof of their own suffering.

I joined Medica soon after the group was founded in April 1993. Medica started as a women's therapy center that focused on providing medical and psycho-social care to women survivors of rape in the war in Bosnia-Herzegovina. Medica was the only organization in Bosnia-Herzegovina which was open to all women survivors of violence no matter what their ethnic background. At that time, everybody—including the media and various branches of government—were searching for testimonies of war violence, genocide and rape. They were searching for proof, but no one was offering any support or direct assistance to the women themselves. Effectively, the rape of women in war had become politicized and sensationalized by the warring states and the international community.

The same thing happened with the Kosovo conflict. Journalists appeared in the refugee camps in Albania holding up signs written in English and Albanian that said: "Searching for a victim of rape who can speak English." All of this was at the expense of supporting individual women in getting through their trauma. Women's suffering was claimed by the states as their own—not just in Bosnia, but in all the countries of former Yugoslavia. Then, with the peace, violence against women became a private matter again and the state lost interest.

Although Medica was established to support women survivors of war violence, the principles we developed at that time still apply. This is because women who suffer violence at the hands of men experience the same trauma, whether the violence occurs during armed conflict or in times of so-called peace.

## A Lack of Services for Violence Survivors

Medica's services, which include medical care, psycho-social care, an SOS-hotline, and educational programs for women, were available to women survivors of domestic violence, incest and rape. By talking to women, our therapists have discovered and actually confirmed something we already knew—that there are no adequate public services to which they can turn except Medica. Although we are working on different projects which are not all necessarily direct services for women, the women of Medica all share the following principles:

- to relate to each woman as a human being, not thinking about her as a victim but rather as a survivor of violence;
- to extend our solidarity and unconditional trust to all women;
- to provide women with psychotherapeutic support, without asking them to prove their stories—women do not have to earn the right to receive our help;
- to protect women from sensationalism, political exploitation, or other forces which do not directly help in their recovery;
- to promote a woman's right to choose and to support and help women to achieve that right;
- to offer help to women regardless of their nationality.

### Taking Action on Violence in Society

Other principles we share are the beliefs that each honest human engagement has its own therapeutic impact and that this work plays an indispensable role in the broader community work. It was obvious to us that we needed to deal with personal problems by doing one-to-one advising and counseling while also starting to take broader action on gender-based violence in society.

For the action aimed at society, we needed to target institutions, the media and society as a whole. To start a campaign against violence against women was not possible without official statistics and data and these were not available from any governmental institution. Since it is Medica's policy not to use clients' personal stories for public purposes, we started to search for official statistics and any kind of data related to violence against women.

We found there was nothing, so in 1997, Infoteka—which was one of the Medica projects—began a research project about violence against women. The study was conducted in 1998 in Zenica, which is a city seventy kilometers north of Sarajevo, that has a population of about 150,000. The project was carried out with the support of UNIFEM's Trust Fund and OXFAM-U.K. & I. The results of the research are not surprising. They are the justification for something we already knew, but for which we did not have proof before. We interviewed a random sample of 542 women. Twenty to 24 percent said they had experienced some form of violence from a partner and 24 percent had experienced physical violence. Only 40 percent had contacted institutions about the problem—the police, the Center for Social Work or the courts. The findings of this research were published by Infoteka in the book *To Live Without Violence*, which is available in both the Bosnian language and English.

We began bombarding the media with findings from the study. Violence against women in so-called peacetime became a public issue. Medica's basic principles are partly implemented to thaw the frozen structures of the institutions. We are in the process of reaching our goal.

### Providing Education for Professionals

A pilot project, which is an educational program in our community, was begun in Zenica in October 1999. Its main goal is to take a multidisciplinary approach in combating violence against women and to improve the work of professionals in governmental institutions. Although we have had very good contacts with individuals working in governmental institutions in the past, it takes a long time and hard work to establish official agreement about education for professionals working in those institutions. The institutions involved are the police department (police officers and inspectors), the health department (doctors and nurses), the court system (judges and public prosecutors), the social department (social workers, lawyers and other professionals), non-governmental institutions and some individuals, such as private practice lawyers and journalists.

The program has received support from the Office of the High Commissioner for Human Rights. Every group received the same educational program, which includes training by psychologists/therapists from Medica. The training includes forms and mechanisms of violence, trauma and its consequences, communication techniques, burnout and how to prevent it and similar issues. The Central and East European Law Initiative of the American Bar Association and the International Criminal Investigative Training Assistance Program, which are international organizations present in Bosnia, will now do further trainings which will include investigation and prosecuting procedures in cases of domestic violence and sexual abuse.

After we did the training with police officers, they realized that there is a need to have a woman present when survivors are giving testimony. They are trying to find professional women who are willing to do this job but it is not easy, as this type of work is new for women in our society. It represents a revolutionary change. The officer at the reception desk, as well as the officer on duty, receive a list of people that we have trained, and are given precise instructions: "If a woman comes, do not question her. Send her to one of them." A small room has been reserved for survivors of violence, where they can wait with someone who will comfort them. In general, a woman will not be made to wait too long, as these cases are now given high priority. So you can imagine how it was before.

A participant in the training of judges and prosecutors stated, "For the first time in my professional life, I had the opportunity to speak about problems and my own powerlessness that I faced at work. For the first time in my life, someone has opened the path of overcoming secondary traumatization and professional stress, which could very much influence the quality and professionalism of my work."

Now, seven months later, the program is still in progress and the results are already significant. It is not difficult to see the changes in the police department, the Center for Social Work and the courts with regard to the attitudes of professionals and their cooperation with each other and with Medica, which has come to be recognized as an equal partner. The pilot project is showing very good success and the other municipalities in Bosnia-Herzegovina would like to implement it as well. We are more than willing, as one of the purposes of the pilot project was to see if it would be possible to implement similar programs in other parts of Bosnia-Herzegovina.

## Challenges

One problem the pilot project faces has been the attitude of leaders in the institutions and the ministers in charge of the various departments. They have shown reluctance to allow the training as they feel they have had their own kind of professional training and don't like to hear that they are not doing their job well. We very much want to have full cooperation with these governmental institutions. We want them to choose to be a part of the project, not only as receivers of training, but as full participants in all activities so that they will feel that this project is theirs as well.

It is difficult to explain to them that we are not interfering with their professional duties, but offering additional skills, and that it is up to them if and when they implement them in their work. We are slowly establishing this kind of relationship through the individuals and groups that we have already trained. They are now spreading the word about what we are doing—how good and important it is—and we are becoming one group headed in the same direction. This is why the assessment period is taking longer than we had expected. However, the results have been much more effective in the end.

Another way of addressing these issues has been through the media and our public campaign against violence against women. It has been successful because we created it with a network of journalists who were personally interested in our work, even if the cost to them was conflict with their editors. We not only speak about women's right to live without violence, but also about women's rights and issues in general, as well as human rights. This is the very best, and really the only way to keep the attention of the media and the public.

## Conclusions

The state, through its institutions, must take responsibility for prosecuting the perpetrators of violence against women. It must ensure the training of police, the judiciary, health workers, and others involved. It must ensure that there is support for women to overcome the trauma of violence. It must actively seek to create a society in which violence against women is seen as unacceptable and wrong.

This problem is not particular to Bosnia-Herzegovina; it exists in all states, no matter how developed they like to perceive themselves to be. Violence against women, unless properly prosecuted by the state, is a human rights violation, and we shall continue to say so.

The message I would like to drive home is that violence against women does not belong in the private domain as a matter of the relationship between the perpetrator and the victim. Violence is a product of the beliefs in a society. A society in which violence against women is condoned, and in some circumstances legally justified by the state, is not a safe place for women.

# Organizing for Sexual Rights: The Namibian Women's Manifesto

Elizabeth Khaxas

*Elizabeth Khaxas is Director of Sister Namibia, an autonomous, non-governmental women's organization based in Windhoek, Namibia. She has worked as a Gender Programme Officer at the newly established gender desk at the South African Development Community (SADC) in Gaborone, Botswana. She has also been a teacher and a school principal.*

*Sister Namibia coordinates a women's resource center that collects materials on women's and gender issues. The organization also conducts research and provides training for women in a number of areas and publishes a bi-monthly magazine called "Sister Namibia."*

NAMIBIA IS A COUNTRY IN SOUTHERN AFRICA WHICH GAINED independence in 1990. Namibia has a democratic constitution based on the principles of equality, human rights and freedom. In fact, the first sentence of the preamble states that recognition of the inherent dignity and of the equal and inalienable rights of all members of the human family is indispensable for freedom, justice and peace. However, this does not mean that the human rights of all Namibians are respected in practice. In fact, many citizens still do not know that they have human rights and what these rights are. Women, in particular, need information and education on their human rights and need to acquire the skills to claim these rights.

However, while our government claims to acknowledge and respect the human rights of all women in general, lesbian women in Namibia are regularly told by our government leaders that they have no human rights at all. The attacks against lesbian and gay people in Namibia began in 1995, shortly after the outburst by Robert Mugabe, President of Zimbabwe, who stated that homosexuals were worse than pigs and dogs. This discourse was taken up in Namibia by senior government leaders, who made statements such as, "Homosexuality is like cancer or AIDS and everything should be done to stop its spread in Namibia," and, "Homosexuality is an unnatural behavior, a behavior disorder which is alien to African culture." Even the president of Namibia publicly condemned homosexuality as "exploiting our democracy" and called for it to be uprooted from Namibian society.

This hate speech creates an atmosphere of fear, considering that sodomy between men is still illegal in Namibia, while the same sexual practice is not criminalized between a man and a woman. We do not yet have equality for all members of the human family, not even in the law books. In fact, in 1998 the Minister of Home Affairs stated in Parliament that his ministry was preparing legislation to ban homosexuality altogether.

Sister Namibia was the first organization in our country that became active in defending the human rights of lesbian and gay people, and we would like to share our experiences with you today. We are an autonomous non-governmental women's organization, which was founded in 1989 on the eve of independence with the following aims: To increase awareness among women, men and young people of the ways in which political, social, cultural, legal and economic systems of power control girls and women; and to oppose and challenge racism, sexism, homophobia and other discourses and practices that divide and oppress people. We utilize our bimonthly magazine, *Sister Namibia*, to promote the human rights of all women, including lesbian women. We also run a resource center that collects materials on women and gender issues. Furthermore, we conduct research and run training programs on women's leadership, human rights and HIV/AIDS.

## The Namibian Women's Manifesto

Last year, Sister was given the mandate to compile a document called *The Namibian Women's Manifesto,* in collaboration with women and some men from women's and human rights NGOs, women in Parliament and all levels of government, political parties and individual women activists. We agreed to compile the *Women's Manifesto* in order to unite women's voices in holding government accountable to the implementation of the national gender policy and the many international conventions on gender and human rights it has signed since independence. *The Namibian Women's Manifesto* aims to mobilize women to participate in elections as candidates and as voters, and to place women's issues on the national agenda. It covers women's human rights in areas such as democracy, education, health and reproductive rights, the economy, the environment and the media.

Women from all major political parties participated actively in the drafting of the *Women's Manifesto*. However, at the time of going to print, the ruling party, SWAPO, withdrew its support because the document made references to the human rights of lesbian women. Allow me to read you the relevant two sentences from the twenty-five-page document that has been used by the ruling party to undermine the women's united call for the human rights of all women. I quote:

> *The human rights of all women, as guaranteed in the Namibian Constitution, need to be ensured, including the rights of the girl child, women living under customary law, women in marginalized ethnic groups, sex workers, disabled women, old women and lesbian women.*

and:

> *We advocate that political parties state their policies on human rights, including violence against women and children, the rights of gay and lesbian people and customary practices that are harmful to women and children.*

## Lesbian and Gay People's Human Rights Not Recognized

The SWAPO Party Women's Council called a press conference just before the launching of the *Women's Manifesto* stating that it was confusing the Namibian women because the rights of lesbian women were, in their view, not a gender issue. This stand was already taken by our government leaders in the preparations for the World Conference on Women in Beijing, where the Namibian delegation was instrumental in keeping references to sexual orientation out of the Platform for Action. In contrast to this narrow definition of gender, we believe that issues of sexuality and sexual orientation are central to an understanding of gender. A further attack on the *Women's Manifesto* came from the Director General of the Department of Women's Affairs, who heads the newly established Ministry for Women's Affairs and Child Welfare. At a meeting of elected women from different political parties, she stated:

> *The so-called* Women's Manifesto *being circulated has no other message than asking women in Namibia to promote homosexuality. The same document calls for comprehensive sexuality education to be introduced into our schools, which is nothing more than a call for our children to be taught how to become gays and lesbians.*

However, the call for comprehensive sexuality education in the *Manifesto* was made with reference to the high rate of AIDS infection in Namibia, which is the third highest in the world. We have regions in Namibia in which 50 percent of the people are already infected with the virus and the majority are girls and women. Are the Namibian people destined to die out for lack of comprehensive sexuality education because of the homophobia of our Minister of Women's Affairs and other top politicians? Not if Sister Namibia can help it.

### An Organizing and Lobbying Tool

In spite of the withdrawal of support for the *Manifesto* by the ruling party and the Department of Women's Affairs, many women in the thirteen regions of Namibia rallied around the *Manifesto* and used it as a tool to mobilize women on human rights issues. In the regional workshops, the issue of human rights of gay and lesbian people came up time and again and this led us to discuss the history of the development of the concept of human rights.

We explained that in 1948 it was mainly white middle-class men from Western countries sitting at the table to draft the United Nations Universal Declaration of Human Rights. This meant that violations of women's human rights through domestic abuse and rape, for example, were not part of the agenda. However, over the years more and more marginalized groups have joined the table to call for their rights as human beings—for example, ethnic minorities and indigenous people, differently-abled people, children, women, lesbian and gay people. Thus, the concept of human rights is expanding as our knowledge and understanding of specific forms of human rights violations grows.

The rural women attending our workshops in all regions of Namibia were pleased to learn that they had human rights not granted to them by the government of the day, but by virtue of being human. They said that this knowledge would empower them to stand up more strongly against domestic violence and harmful cultural practices and to assert their own dignity. By the same token, an overwhelming majority did not hesitate in embracing the human rights of lesbian women and having this included in "their" *Manifesto*. Without prompting, they came up with arguments against the ruling party on this issue. They made statements such as:

> *The Minister did not ask us for our views on this issue. Lesbian women are our mothers, sisters, and daughters. We cannot just throw them out. They are taxpayers like everyone else, and have the same rights as everyone else.*

They even included these arguments in humorous role-plays, practicing how to bring the *Women's Manifesto* to their communities and sat up half the night debating these issues. Thus, *The Namibian Women's Manifesto* has become a lobbying tool for all women's human rights, including the rights of lesbian women, far beyond the expectations of its authors. It has also contributed to breaking the silence on issues of women's sexuality, which is so crucial for the prevention of unwanted pregnancy and HIV/AIDS. The *Women's Manifesto* Network is currently fundraising for and starting new projects in the areas of women's leadership, women's human rights, and women and HIV/AIDS.

**Lesbians Denied Full Human Rights**

When we campaign for the human rights of lesbian women, what do we mean? Take my case as an example: I have lived with my partner for ten years and we are raising our son together. Yet, we have no legal rights to live together as a family because we are two women and my partner is not a Namibian citizen. Her application for permanent residence has been rejected twice by the Ministry of Home Affairs without reasons given. Fortunately, a public interest law firm has taken up our case as a human rights issue, and we won a victory in June last year when the High Court of Namibia ordered the Ministry of Home Affairs to grant my partner permanent residence within thirty days.

The court recognized our relationship as a universal partnership, just like any heterosexual couple living together in community of property, but without a marriage license. However, the government has appealed against this decision and the case will be heard by the Supreme Court in October 2000. In the meantime, the Ministry of Home Affairs has not even renewed my partner's work permit, thus putting our life together on tenuous hold. Will we have to seek political refuge in South Africa, our southern neighbor, which has enshrined the human rights of lesbian and gay people in its 1994 constitution and has recently ordered the Ministry of Home Affairs to grant permanent residence to foreign partners of lesbian and gay citizens? This will be our last resort as we plan to stay put and continue our struggle for our rights as lesbian women in Namibia, including the rights to adoption, joint medical aid and pension fund, and the many other rights and benefits accorded to heterosexual couples. We are here to speak out in support of all lesbian women denied their human rights the world over, and we speak with the voices of many urban and rural women in Namibia who have understood that human rights are indivisible.

# Redefining and Confronting "Honor Killings" as Femicide

Nadera Shalhoub-Kevorkian

*Nadera Shalhoub-Kevorkian is a Palestinian therapist and activist, who works with the Jerusalem-based Women's Center for Legal Aid and Counseling. She is a professor of criminology and social work at Hebrew University. In 1994, she initiated the first hotline in the West Bank and Gaza for Palestinian women who are experiencing abuse, including femicide, in which women are threatened with death for supposed transgressions to "family honor." Honor accusations are nearly always leveled at a woman's sexuality and may be activated if it becomes known that a woman has experienced sexual abuse, including rape or incest, or if she is suspected of being involved in a romantic relationship.*

*Nadera Shalhoub-Kevorkian has been instrumental in redefining the concept of so-called honor killing by replacing it with the term "femicide," which she says better describes the situation from the women's perspective. She has also broadened the concept of femicide to include the state in which a woman's life is constantly threatened and limited in numerous ways while she is under suspicion or accused of "honor" violations. Shalhoub-Kevorkian refers to this state as "living death."*

*The Women's Center for Legal Aid and Counseling (WCLAC) uses a variety of innovative strategies when attempting to save women from being killed by family members. These may include round-the-clock accompaniment, providing the woman with a cellular phone so that she can contact help at any moment, and intensive counseling and negotiation sessions with the family. Tribal and government authorities are also approached and appealed to in an effort to enlist their support in preventing the killing from taking place. The WCLAC has pioneered the use of signed agreements with family members and local authorities, in which families agree not to kill the woman while other solutions to the problem are being sought. The WCLAC has made progress in opening discussions with the various levels of authority operating in the region about how to deal with the issue of femicide.*

I AM A PALESTINIAN ACTIVIST, THERAPIST, AND RESEARCHER. I WORK with the hotline service of the Women's Center for Legal Aid and Counseling (WCLAC), which serves women in the Palestinian Authority area. I've been on the hotline since 1994 but I've been with the Center since 1990. I was asked to talk to you about new ideas and new strategies and innovative methods for dealing with abuses inflicted upon women. This presentation deals with what I call "The Valley of Death," in which females perceived to have violated the so-called honor code are forced to enter its doors and are condemned to experience a living death.

### Taking Action, Confronting Injustice

I never believed in the statement: "There is nothing to be done about this crime. This is our culture and this is our life and we ought to accept it."[1] My position became stronger when I met Laila. Laila is a fourteen-year-old girl who was raped by her thirty-five-year-old cousin. She was told by the whole family that the best way to deal with the scandal—or what I term the crime and abuse—would be for her to marry the man. Her father said, and I quote:

> *The first thing that crossed my mind when I learned that she was raped was to kill her. And you don't know. I still might end up losing my mind and killing her. The whole village learned about the rape and the cousin—the rapist—was kind to us. He was kind to us and agreed to marry her. This is the best way of coping with this catastrophe that she brought to this family.*

Her mother said:

> *It is such a shameful thing, something that people in this village will never forget and they will never forgive this family. It has brought so much pain to the whole family. I wish she had died rather than putting us in such a shameful state.*

Laila was looking at me with very sad eyes, but she never said a word. In her eyes, there was fear, sadness and pain. I tried to talk with her but how could I dialogue with this voice that had been muted for years? How could I dialogue with a person that was silent and had been both socialized and acculturated in such a way that silence was the only language she could speak? How could I make her say what she needed when it was impossible?

Six months later and after her marriage to this rapist—after the crime of this marriage was imposed on her—she came back and wanted to talk to me. She sneaked out of her house and village, saying she was going to the gynecologist, and managed to reach me. The first thing she said when she saw me was that I was the only hope left for her and that she wanted to talk. She said the unspeakable. She said that she had tried many times during the last six months to commit suicide, but had failed to do so. She said:

> *Would you believe it, Nadera, that I was even scared to take my own life? I feel that they all raped me—my mother, my parents that were supposed to protect me and help me—they all abandoned me. I became a slave to the one who raped me and now I'm pregnant with his baby. Death is nothing compared to my life these days.*

The reality is that women are killed for so-called honor reasons, or what is termed "crimes of family honor." So many women were not as "lucky" as Laila. They were killed for being victims of incest, rape, alleged adultery, "ill repute" behavior. So many women, after surviving the abusive ordeal of the "honor accusation" have been made to live in the Valley of Death. My presentation is about the right to live in the Valley of Life. As the poet Khalil Gibran said:

> *Just as a single leaf does not turn yellow without the silent knowledge of the whole tree,*
> *So the wrong doers cannot do wrong without the hidden will of you all.*

## Complicity at Many Levels

When I started studying femicide—and, again, I call it "femicide" because it is woman killing, which is the way we decided to define it at the Center—we found that it wasn't only the actual killing we were confronting. Femicide is a process. The end of the process is death—the medical, legal death. But the beginning of this process involves all sorts of methods of killing that start with threats and hardships after a woman has been a victim of abuse, or incest, or all sorts of sexual and physical abuses and suppositions, or because someone supposes that *maybe* she is having a relationship. I decided that although the classical definition of femicide is the actual death, Laila and so many other women that I worked with and studied explained that they are, as one of them—a seventeen-year-old who was raped by her brother—told me, "living death."

We decided that the work would be on femicide cases—not only those women who were actually killed, but also those who were under the threat of being killed. And I am sorry to say that three of my clients ended up being killed by the end of the study.[2] According to the Forensic Medicine Officer's report, their deaths were termed "suicide" or "natural death." In this work I learned that death is the inability to live. Society has imposed on many girls like Laila, forcing them to marry the rapist in an attempt to "cleanse" the shame inflicted on the family. Others were asked to marry an older man, a mentally sick or retarded man, or kept in home imprisonment or home confinement just to safeguard the so-called family honor.

In addition, we learned that many women were killed but there was no documentation that stated they were victims of such a crime. We learned during this research that the *muqtars*—heads of clans—were writing death certificates. In one of the interviews with a muqtar, his wife showed me a death certificate. It showed the woman's name and age, which, in this case, was twenty-seven, and gave the cause of death as "old age." He didn't even try to find a better reason.

For many women, instead of saying they were killed, they say that they fell in the well. Do you know how many women "fell in the well?" Do you know how hard it is to know that you know very well that somebody has killed them? When trying to learn more about such atrocities, we found out that the conspiracy of silence is criminal. Not only the family members killed her, but also the tribal heads who were addressed to help in solving the problem. They felt that the best way to handle crimes against family honor was killing. When interviewing the tribal heads, they were very helpful in explaining to me the various methods of killing women. They told me that killing women "is as easy as drinking water. There are so many ways of killing women," they said.

When we saw that the family and the tribal heads were that abusive, we decided to go to the criminal justice personnel and to the criminal justice records, and what we found was worse. I don't know what the real number of such crimes is. The criminal justice records were so awful that it was hard to know the real number of deaths.

After starting the femicide project we decided that we couldn't sit and wait until the legal system changes, or the social law regarding shame and honor was altered. We saw we needed to help those who feel they are under the threat of being killed to survive. We created a model of intervention, which I call "blocking her exclusion." This model offers strategies that use and activate potential resources in every case and help to prevent the killing. The model allowed us to open a dialogue, not only with the victim, but also with her family, during which we search for methods of supporting and helping her without jeopardizing her life. In doing so, I first map the existing resources. Then I search for those who could help me help the victim, and sign a written agreement with them. The written commitment makes them first and foremost acknowledge that an act of abuse has occurred, and that we ought to take responsibility and deal with it. This model allows us to do intensive support and follow up, while opening new alternatives to help both victims and families. This model uses various existing resources, including governors, police officers, extended family members, tribal notables, clergy people and others, all of whom are convinced to safeguard the victim.

### Admitting Abuse, Accepting Responsibility

This method involves opening a dialogue with the governor in order to help us, and opening a dialogue with the tribal head and with clergy people that would help us work together in order to safeguard the woman's life. They are supposed to sign an agreement, which says that they agree on the fact that nobody should kill her and that "we will work from here, because she is a victim." This way, they at least acknowledge the fact that the woman has been a victim of abuse.[3]

This model allowed us to do intensive support and follow-up while opening new alternatives and helping both the victim and the family cope with the problem. It helped us to use various existing resources in order to solve the problem. Most cases of femicide that came to the Women's Center for Legal Aid and Counseling were in a very bad and harsh situation and it was almost impossible to prevent the killings. Some of them came when they were eight months pregnant. Some women reached us after being imprisoned for a long time. How can you help an incest victim who has been imprisoned for three years in order to protect her from being killed by her own family members?[4] Some came to us after losing their virginity, which could bring about their death if discovered. Others were threatened with being killed just because someone in the family suspected they were in love with someone. Therefore, we felt that in addition to the intervention model, we needed a prevention strategy through which we could dialogue with those who had been muted for years so that they could disclose the abuse they had experienced in a manner that would prevent their being killed.

We started a new program which we called the Dialogue Tent. In the Dialogue Tent, we tried to reach those women who had never contacted the Center's hot line, trying to see if there were also cases of women who were under the threat of being killed, which we might be able to prevent. If they had been sexually abused, maybe we could intervene before it was too late. We started the Dialogue Tent in different areas in the West Bank.

Let me conclude by saying that there is a need for governments to look properly at those cases. There is a need for state officials to know that this is their role and they should be more responsible. We need to try to change the legal system. Our legal system is not "our" legal system.[5] The challenges and dilemmas that face us when working with such abuses are very, very hard. Human experiences, hardships, and oppressions are not static, but rather the material used by men and women to create history. When we learn how to read and understand, we no longer remain dead weight in a cooperating world, but rather creators, molders and innovators of culture.

### Creating a Platform for Dialogue

I speak to you in the hope that this presentation will serve to create an open platform for dialogue that is based on sharing experiences, rather than imposing concepts and imprisoning our thinking with what is seen by some Western researchers as fundamental scientific evidence and feminist, ideological or political "musts."[6] The question is how to bring about changes when the political structure and the powerful groups consider women *persona non grata*.

How can we, as human rights activists, work on empowering women when all social, political, religious and cultural forces oppress, discriminate and silence us?

We believe in revolutionary cultural, political, social action that promotes growth. I believe in growth that takes into consideration what exists and builds on it. Growth also means to identify and empower those who are able to carry on the struggle and never to impose it on those who are powerless and possess meager resources. The question is, how can we close the gates of the Valley of Death? Are we able to talk about the rights of the individual to live? I would like to finish by quoting what Ghalil Gibran once said:

> *They tell me "If you see a slave asleep, do not awaken him lest he dreams of freedom." But I tell them "If I see a slave asleep, I will awaken him and talk to him about freedom and help him to reach freedom."*

# Notes

1. Nadera Shalhoub-Kevorkian makes it clear that femicide or "honor killing" is not a concept contained in the Koran, but rather an act based on patriarchal attitudes in society. She has also stated that the use of the term "traditional practice" in recent United Nations discourse is problematic because it works against efforts by groups like the WCLAC to put an end to destructive actions like femicide, by assigning them with a level of respect and legitimacy that they do not deserve (Conversation with Nadera Shalhoub-Kevorkian, December 2000).

2. Between 1996 and 1998, the Women's Center for Legal Aid and Counseling carried out an intensive study of the incidence and characteristics of femicide in Palestine. Nadera Shalhoub-Kevorkian, *Mapping and Analyzing the Landscape of Femicide in Palestinian Society* (January 2000).

3. Conversations with family members and local authorities demonstrate that families feel the woman is to blame for the dishonor a sexual crime brings on the family, regardless of the fact that she has been a victim of abuse. The WCLAC's approach is innovative in that it seeks to change this outlook by appealing to family members and authorities to view the woman as a victim who deserves protection and support, rather than punishment. The process provides the WCLAC with time to seek a solution to the problem that does not include killing the woman. ibid.

4. The standard practice whereby police can protect a woman from being killed is to incarcerate her. Some women remain in protective custody for years without the situation being resolved. According to Nadera Shalhoub-Kevorkian, this practice is also part of the femicide experience, as the woman, although technically alive, becomes unable to live her life. She claims that people have tended to underestimate the emotional burden that is placed on women in this situation and says it is possible to equate the honor accusation experience with being on Death Row (Conversation with Nadera Shalhoub-Kevorkian, December 2000).

5. Due to the long-term colonial experience of Palestine, no coherent overall legal system exists. Two main jurisdictions are in place, each with overlapping layers of historic legislation and customary law that have not been standardized. In the Gaza Strip, the law is based on the Egyptian system, which, in turn, is heavily influenced by French law. The West Bank uses the Jordanian system, which is based on British law and earlier law from the Ottoman Empire. The entire region is influenced by earlier colonization by the Ottoman Empire as well as Napoleonic and Islamic law. Israeli military orders are in use whenever occupying forces decide to apply them (Conversation with Nadera Shalhoub-Kevorkian, December 2000).

6. Nadera Shalhoub-Kevorkian and the WCLAC have been criticized by some sectors for their broad use of the term "femicide," which they apply not only to women who have literally been killed, but to those whose lives have been defined by the honor accusation. They therefore include women in the definition of femicide who have been forced to marry their abusers or who have been imprisoned in their homes or in jails, supposedly to prevent their being killed (Conversation with Nadera Shalhoub-Kevorkian, December 2000).

# The Tokyo Tribunal: Confronting Rape and Sexual Violence as War Crimes

Indai Sajor

*Indai Lourdes Sajor is the founder and Executive Director of the Asian Center for Women's Human rights (ASCENT). Her work with the human rights systems includes monitoring, investigation, documentation, reporting, and enforcing women's human rights. She has been active in working towards recognition of rape and sexual violence as war crimes and crimes against humanity. She is one of the conveners of the International Organizing Committee for the Women's International War Crimes Tribunal on Japan's Military Sexual Slavery, which took place in Tokyo in December 2000.*

*The Women's International War Crimes Tribunal (also known as the Tokyo Tribunal) is a people's tribunal organized by Asian women and human rights organizations with the support of international NGOs, to hear cases of sexual slavery and other crimes involving sexual violence committed against women during World War II, by the Japanese Army. The Tribunal, which took place December 8–12, 2000, was designed to serve as a public hearing for women from Korea, Indonesia, Japan, and the Netherlands who were forced into sexual slavery by the military. Besides providing a forum for hearing evidence on the nature of the crimes committed against the "comfort women" (as they were euphemistically referred to by the army), it was hoped that the Tribunal would aid in the process of creating an international movement to support the work women are doing on violence against women in war and armed conflict situations. The Women's International War Crimes Tribunal was followed by a one-day hearing on current war crimes, with presentations by women from Latin America, Africa, Asia and parts of former Yugoslavia.*

LOLA TOMASA SALINOG IS NOW SEVENTY-SIX YEARS OLD. SHE IS from the Philippines and a former comfort woman. She was fourteen years old when the Japanese Imperial Army abducted her during the Second World War. This is her story:

*They entered our house late in the evening by forcibly pushing the door open. My father and I woke up from our sleep. One of the soldiers grabbed me and dragged me out of the house. My father tried to stop them by holding them back. Then one of the soldiers got angry and pulled out his sword and hit my father in the head. He hit my father so hard that his head was cut off and rolled on the floor. I tried to pick it up but was terrified. Then the soldiers dragged me out of the house and brought me to the garrison, where I was raped many times that night. I was thinking of my dead father when they raped me. My mother died when I was one month old and it was my father who brought me up. We were really close. I stayed in the garrison for almost a year and every morning and evening the soldiers would line up and use me. I would be so weak and many times bleeding.*

Let me share another story with you. This is about a girl from Sierra Leone. She said:

*We went to find wood and potato leaves in a village called Mathiaka. One of the soldiers grabbed me. I got away but then more of them came and surrounded us. They beat me and hit me hard on the back of the neck with a gun. The one who caught me made me pound rice and wash his clothes and he was the one who had sex with me. I begged him to let me go to my people, but he said, "I'm going to have sex with you until they disarm us." He kept saying he would kill me if ever I tried to get away. I was with him for twenty days.*

These are the words of an eleven-year-old girl who was abducted by the rebel forces on January 25, 2000, when she left an internally-displaced camp near Partook, Northern Province of Sierra Leone.

The story of Lola Tomasa happened during the Second World War, between 1941 and 1942. The story of the young girl from Sierra Leone happened earlier this year. The same violence that happened to women fifty-five years ago is still happening today, and impunity prevails to this day.

**Recognizing the Impact of War**

Here are the hard facts of the ravages of war and its impact on women, men and children: Over the past decade armed conflict has killed 2 million children, disabled 5 million and left 12 million homeless. Every month more than 2,000 people are killed or maimed by mine explosions. Although around 100,000 mines were removed in 1994, two million more were planted the following year. The number of refugees alone has increased dramatically. In 1960 there were 2.5 million refugees. By 1996 there were more than 16 million refugees around the world, 80 percent of them women and children. Sudan, for example, has 4 million internally displaced people and 730,000 refugees from other countries. There are 100,000 East Timorese who are still living in refugee camps in West Timor. Thousands of ethnic minorities are trying to survive on the borders and in refugee camps in Thailand. War and armed conflict has brought unbearable suffering and horrendous human rights violations, and the number of conflicts continues to grow.

This is the global context in which we launched the Campaign for Justice for the Asian Comfort Women. I would like to reflect on how it all began by illustrating the local struggles and the global options, the solidarity campaigns, and the use of global mechanisms and global mobilizations in demanding justice and reparation for the former comfort women.

**Raising Legal Challenges**

What have we done?

Since 1993 we have filed court cases against the Japanese government at the Tokyo District Court. With the *pro bono* assistance of the Japanese lawyers and solidarity groups in Japan we were able to file court cases with the former comfort women as plaintiffs. To date, seven court cases have been filed in Japan by women from South and North Korea, China, Taiwan, the Philippines, and the Netherlands who became comfort women in Indonesia during the Second World War. In 1998, the Filipino and the Dutch case were both lost at the Tokyo District Court. But we have decided to appeal the cases to the highest court in Tokyo. One of the campaigns that brought us all together is that we have picketed the Japanese Embassy in most of the victimized countries. The Korean comfort women, for example, have been picketing the Japanese Embassy in Seoul since 1992. Every Wednesday they go in front of the embassy and picket. In all these years, they have only missed two pickets because of snow storms and floods and their weekly presence has become a broad movement in Korea. One of the things that we were able to achieve through our campaign is that the issue of the comfort women will be included in Japanese textbooks.

We have also brought the issue of the comfort women to the Commission on Human rights in Geneva. We were able to get the United Nations Special Rapporteur on Violence Against Women, Radhika Coomaraswamy, and the United Nations Rapporteur on Slavery and Slavery-Like Practices, Gay McDougal, to give a report and make recommendations to take the Japanese government to task for their wartime accountability and responsibility to the comfort women during World War II. The comfort women campaign has helped to build recognition that sexual slavery is a serious human rights violation and established the basis for the prohibition of sexual slavery in the Statutes of the International Criminal Court. The statute defines sexual slavery as a war crime and a crime against humanity.

The lessons we learned from the comfort women helped us define the elements of this crime. The comfort women have changed core concepts in international law. Many human rights defenders, historians, lawyers, and academics have dedicated their time to documenting and analyzing their cases. Through their work, for example, we were able to demonstrate that more than one crime was committed against each individual woman. The women suffered not only sexual slavery, but also rape, torture, forced pregnancy, forced sterilization, abduction, enforced prostitution, mutilation, inhumane treatment, murder, and genocide. The failure of the Japanese government and the international community to bring the perpetrators to justice has inflicted additional suffering on the women.

### The Tribunal

It is in this context that we are organizing the Women's International War Crimes Tribunal on Japan's military sexual slavery this coming December in Tokyo. We are also going to have a one-day public hearing on recent and current war crimes, so that we will be able to link the past war crimes that have been committed to the current war crimes that are continuing to this day. We choose to convene a tribunal as a means of giving the former comfort women the sense of justice that has long been denied them, by making their suffering visible and exposing the perpetrators.

The former comfort women from the victimized countries and human rights defenders have been working for the past year in preparation for the Tokyo Tribunal. Our specific objectives are:

1. to involve the international community in exposing the crimes committed against the comfort women of Asia and identifying the steps to be taken against the Japanese government;
2. to create an international movement to address violence against women in armed conflict; and
3. to end impunity for sexual violence against women in wartime and prevent such crimes from happening in the future.

The Tokyo Tribunal will include international prosecutors from each victimized country and a panel of eminent judges from around the world. Our goal is to expand international and humanitarian law to insure accountability, not only for the individual perpetrators, but also the states that directed the abuse.

For the first time, fifty comfort women from the victimized countries will participate in the tribunal. We have decided to bring these women, most of whom are advanced in age, to Tokyo for this very important event so that they may see and meet one another. A one-day public hearing on current war crimes will also be conducted after the tribunal so that we can link these past war crimes to the present and learn from the experience.

**Linking the Past with the Future**

Now, let us step back for a moment and recall what brought us all together here. Let us think of all the women survivors of war crimes and the women who are fighting for this cause. Let us focus on the heroic acts of the women who have given us their stories. They took the risk of stigmatization, of opening old wounds and of experiencing profound isolation. Let us ponder for a moment how we, in our work, can bring the results home to individual women. How do we make it worth their struggle and the enormous risks they have taken?

The answer is to look back and to look forward at the same time. We look back and insist that those responsible cannot hide any longer and should be brought to justice. We look forward and do all we can to make sure that no more women are subjected to these horrors, and that whenever women are abused, the perpetrators do not escape unpunished. The heroic acts of the Asian comfort women and other women and men who have been victims of war have inspired us all in many ways, and even changed our lives.

I conclude with a statement from Lola Tomasa Salinog. She said:

*I'm too old. I won't see justice in my lifetime. Many Japanese people have come to me asking for forgiveness for what their forefathers have done to me. But I can die in peace knowing that my story will make changes in the lives of other women long after I am gone.*

## COMMENTARY
# Challenging Resistance to Women's Human Rights

Sunila Abeyesekera

Some of this group of presentations were about sexual rights and reproductive rights and women's right to have access to health care, and others were about women in times of war and conflict. Both of them link very much to the processes that are going on with the Beijing + 5 meeting and the Outcomes Document.

In terms of women's health and particularly sexual and reproductive health, it is one of the areas in which women's groups have done a lot of work around the Beijing conference. Paragraph 96 of the Platform for Action remains, for many of us, definitive, because it talks about the right to have control over and decide freely and responsibly on matters related to our sexuality, including sexual and reproductive health that is free of coercion, discrimination and violence. And, unfortunately, this language and concept is seriously under threat as the Beijing + 5 discussions proceed. Redefining what is private and affirming women's right to choose without interference from the state or from religion or from the community has evolved out of a focus on health as a right, and not as a service or a need that must be fulfilled.

*Sunila Abeyesekere is Executive Director of INFORM, a human rights monitoring and advocacy organization in Sri Lanka. She received the United Nations Human Rights Award in 1998.*

## Erosion of Rights Gained

Adopting a rights-based approach to women's issues was an idea for which women worked during the Beijing conference. It is in this area where we can now see a lot of erosion taking place. We are hearing serious questions being raised all over again, five years later, about whether health is a right, about whether women in particular circumstances have a right to have access to health care, and so forth.

Some of the presentations this afternoon were about women in war and conflict situations and it is very relevant because today, more than ever before, there are more wars and conflict situations around the globe. The issue of honor killings puts a focus on the role that is increasingly being allocated to women as bearers of culture and tradition and honor, and the use of words like "culture" and "tradition" to dilute and erode rights that some women have won after many, many years of struggle.

There are a few things that arose in the context of the presentations that we need to put very firmly on our agenda as we go into the lobbying process tomorrow. One is that the definition of the family is once again at stake. Many refuse to acknowledge the diverse forms of the family, and there is a blindness to the fact that as much as the family is a site of love and caretaking, it is also a site of violence for many women. This review process has a real problem with the issue of diversity, not only in terms of acknowledging the presence of lesbian women, not only in terms of the phrase "sexual orientation," but even in terms of saying "the full diversity of women." There is also resistance to looking at all state obligations in the context of the full diversity of women. It is extremely worrying if reference to diversity disappears from these documents.

## Resisting Accountability

There is growing resistance from states to be accountable and to allow civil society, other states and the international community to hold states accountable for women's human rights. There is a real reluctance to assume the role of protecting and preventing human rights abuse that is committed by actors and agents that are not linked directly to the state. The concept that a state must show due diligence in trying to meet its human rights obligations, which has been developed in human rights practice over a number of years, is often being abandoned. Further, we see an increase in the affirmation of sovereignty by some states, who declare, "Well, it is a part of our sovereign right not to have other people—citizens in our societies and citizens from other societies—telling us that this or that is a violation of human rights."

At the same time, there seems to be a real reluctance on the part of states to put their money where their mouth is and very little is being said at this review in terms of allocation of resources, especially for the provision of services to women, particularly in the area of health.

## Mobilizing Civil Society

I think as we listened to all the women who spoke here today, all of them represent the vitality of civil society. They are based in their own societies and have mobilized thousands of women and men around issues of the human rights of women. So how can we then move forward into a process of reviewing the Beijing Conference and its follow-up in an environment that doesn't have a strategy for including civil society actors and the roles that they can play in the Beijing + 5 Review? It is very important for us to move into the next week with a sense that we have achieved some things that we are not going to let go of, and that there is strength and energy among us that we can use to move forward during the next week to hold onto the positions that we gained in 1995 in Beijing.

COMMENTARY
# The Only Thing We're Asking for is Implementation

*Pierre Sané*

I'D LIKE TO TALK ABOUT THREE LESSONS I DREW FROM THIS ROUND of presentations before saying a few words on the state of preparations for the UN Special Session.

The first one is the importance of researching and accurately documenting individual cases of human rights abuses. As shown in the case of the Peru experience, it is very important to document individual cases as professionally as possible in order to be able to establish patterns and then demand government responsibility. It is this professional work that has allowed the Peruvian NGOs to take their report to the government bodies, to the media, to the Inter-American Court of Human Rights in the cases of the violations committed in the public health sector. That is very important and even if other types of mobilization activities are equally valuable, the starting point is about documenting human rights violations accurately, using the standards that have been agreed on by the governments.

The second step, as shown in the example of Namibia, is to mobilize and educate using a human rights framework. In this case, the *Women's Manifesto* was used to educate and to campaign, not just on women's rights but also on the rights of gays and lesbians, on the issue of HIV and AIDS and on human rights in general. The same is true for the case of Bosnia, where the book on violence against women is used to mobilize and to campaign.

*Pierre Sané is Secretary General of Amnesty International.*

A third comment I would like to make is about the need to hold governments accountable for their failures or for their inaction—their failures to protect the human rights of women, be it in the case of honor killings in Palestine and Jordan, violence against women in Bosnia or the need to end impunity for war crimes, including sexual slavery.

**Leadership and Commitment are Needed**
Now, many men are involved in the UN preparations for Beijing + 5, and it shows in the document that has been produced so far. We are on the eve of the Special Session of the General Assembly, and some basic concepts that were agreed on in Vienna at the World Conference on Human Rights or in Beijing are again being challenged—concepts having to do with women's human rights. The discussion on the theme of the human rights of women in the Outcomes Document to be produced by the UN General Assembly's review of the Beijing Platform for Action this year has been delegated to a group tasked to examine controversial issues arising from this review. While some governments have come with a genuine desire to review implementation of their commitments in 1995, others are bent on undermining the process, including refusing to restate goals for ratification of women's treaties, or even the International Criminal Court—agreements that were reached at previous conferences. For once, it seems that the United States is playing a positive role in insisting on a strong document, but as usual, the legitimacy of the U.S. will be undermined by its failure to ratify the CEDAW convention. I think the U.S. will be in a position to speak with a stronger voice and to listen to others once it has ratified CEDAW and some other key conventions, including the Convention on the Rights of the Child.

Some countries are showing real leadership, and it is encouraging to see governments from Southern Africa and some Latin American countries pushing for strong language—pushing for an honest review of what has been achieved, what are the obstacles, and where do we go from here. At the same time, a handful of governments are playing a very destructive role. A peculiar alliance, which includes Iran, Pakistan, Syria, Nicaragua, the Holy See and Algeria, are trying to hold back the achievements of previous years. We all want a good document—a document that is an honest review of what has been achieved, a document that clearly articulates the obstacles to moving forward, and a document which will really bring the governments to commit themselves to achieving the objectives that were already set out in the Beijing Platform for Action.

We are not here to set new targets. The targets that were set have not been achieved. What we need is to get agreements from the international community that these will be the targets and that these will be the dates by which these targets will be met, so that we can monitor and hold the governments accountable for the implementation of the agreements that they have made. They developed the Platform for Action of Beijing and the Beijing Declaration. The only thing we're asking for is implementation.

## Death Fireworks

Just like a sudden
firework
it comes in
to make your heart
burst
in million colors
Oh, how lucky we are...
they were blasting
All around us,
and we are still alive.
...
Didn't you hear
those goodbyes?
Did you know meaning
of all falling stars?
...
Didn't you hear
that someone cried,
silently,
through all those nights?
against
the madness
of artificial lights,
sent out to burst
our bodies and hearts
in million pieces.

It is too strong,
for strongest minds,
you start to wonder
where your peace
is.

Oh, they were so,
so close to us...
they flew over roofs
and dug out the ground...
you couldn't escape
their screaming
sound–
You couldn't sing
against all those
death fireworks
the bells were dumb,
and couldn't ring

The town knelt
down
and dreamt in its pain–
anything,
just to forget
all beautiful, flowered
gardens
where only pure
soil has left.
...
Didn't you hear
those goodbyes?
Did falling stars mean
that they died?
...
We saw the colors
vanished in night...
And the whole space
silently cried...

*Bojana Blagojevic was born in Gorazde, Bosnia and came to the United States in 1996 to continue her education, which had been interrupted by the war. She attended Rutgers University, where she worked at the Center for Women's Global Leadership. Her poems have been published in magazines, newspapers and anthologies.*

"This poem was written in the United States. It was Independence Day, and I went to see fireworks. They were very beautiful, but the noise they made reminded me of shelling. So I wrote about a different kind of fireworks—death fireworks..."

©Bojana Blagojevic. North Plainfield, July 6, 1996. Reprinted by permission of author.

## Section 2

# Women's Economic Rights: Challenging the Structures of Injustice

THE PRESENTATIONS IN THIS SECTION PROVIDE EXAMPLES OF some of the ways women's economic rights are being violated in societies around the world, and what women are doing to organize against this.

Women's vulnerability to other human rights abuses, including violence, is greatly increased by the limited amount of economic power that they hold. While women do two-thirds of the world's work, they earn only 5 percent of its income. Although the Beijing Platform for Action (PFA) contains sections on women's economic rights and women's poverty, at the time of the Beijing Conference, many women were disappointed that clearer measures were not set out for making concrete progress in this area. At Beijing + 5—largely due to women's organizing—some advances were achieved, as several resolutions that strengthen economic rights in the Platform were brought forth and accepted. (For more information about this, see "Women's Economic Rights: A Few Steps Forward and a Long Way to Go," by elmira Nazombe, on page 173 of this book.)

Women's unpaid labor in their homes and in their communities is not only vital for the maintenance of their societies, but constitutes a substantial (though largely invisible) subsidy to the world's wealth. In the globalized world of today, women can be found concentrated in the lowest paid and least secure jobs, while they continue to carry nearly all the burden of childcare and household upkeep. And although, in some countries, the gap between men's and women's education levels is beginning to close, this is not necessarily reflected in women's wages. Meanwhile, in many countries, women are facing long-term, ingrained attitudes in society that prevent them from accessing education and an equal share of resources. Yet women are discovering ways of fighting economic injustice, and are developing new alliances in the process. Increasingly, women are using human rights instruments to bolster local strategies for gaining economic rights, despite the resistance they often encounter within and beyond their own societies.

The case of the women in Nepal, presented by Sapana Pradhan Malla, shows how women have used the Convention for the Elimination of All Forms of Discrimination against Women (CEDAW) to try to gain the inheritance rights that are denied them. Forbidden by customary and civil law to inherit property from their parents, women organized to sue the government for non-compliance with CEDAW. Their case has sparked heated debate in the country about traditional practices and views that lead to widespread discrimination and devaluing of women and girls.

The presention by Sarah Mukasa of Akina Mama wa Afrika sheds light on the types of injustice refugees are experiencing at this moment when armed conflicts and political and economic crises are causing people to leave their homelands in greater numbers than ever before. Women experience particular kinds of problems when they become refugees and these are being exacerbated as the wealthier countries become increasingly protective of their borders and resources. Women from Africa and other countries of the global South experience racism along with the other, multiple pressures they face as immigrants or refugees. Although the situation described is in the United Kingdom, governments' increasingly punitive response to immigrants and refugees, in the context of a growing world prison industry, needs to be taken into account as a grave human rights issue that must be addressed in many countries.

The case presented by Olga Rivas of Guatemala looks at the situation women face as workers in export processing plants (*maquilas*) that are often owned by multinational corporations. In many countries, women's low wage labor is being used as a means of attracting international investment. Ongoing labor abuses coupled with generalized human rights violations are common characteristics of this form of production. In Central America, women have organized a regional network to confront these abuses and to challenge their governments to honor the human rights agreements they have signed. The issues surrounding the maquila highlight the need to arrive at clear policies on how to hold non-state actors—including multinational corporations—accountable for the human rights violations they commit.

The presentation by Joy Butts of the Kensington Welfare Rights Union (KWRU) provides a look at poverty in the United States today. It shows how, at a moment when the economy is generally regarded as "robust," there are great discrepancies in terms of the distribution of wealth and economic opportunities. The KWRU has taken the groundbreaking step of attempting to sue the U.S. government at the Inter-American Court of Human Rights for violating the economic rights of poor people. Although the case was not accepted for hearing, the group has used the opportunity to educate people on human rights, pointing out that the United States has refused to sign the International Covenant on Economic, Social and Cultural Rights.

The work described in the presentation by Ayesha Imam of Nigeria highlights an innovative project for educating people on women's human rights, beginning with the youngest members of society—the children. In hosting a poster contest, BAOBAB for women's human rights was able to learn a great deal about children's perceptions of human rights, while promoting awareness of women's human rights throughout the country.

The five cases presented in this section are indicative of but a few of the ways women are working to gain the economic justice that has long been denied them. It is also worth remembering that women form an important part of the numerous struggles that are taking place for more generalized economic rights for poor people everywhere. To the extent that they bring gender awareness to this struggle, they are providing these efforts with added strength and the possibility of real structural change in the future.

# Using CEDAW to Fight for Women's Inheritance Rights

Sapana Pradhan Malla

*Sapana Pradhan Malla is a practicing lawyer in the Supreme Court of Nepal. She has been a member of Parliament and works to reform laws and policies that discriminate against women in her country. She is involved in the Asia-Pacific Forum for Women, Law and Development and International Women's Rights Action Watch (IWRAW) Asia-Pacific, Equality Now, and other national and international associations. She participates in the multilevel campaign by Nepalese women to change legislation that denies women the right to inherit property from their families and was legal council in the case that brought the issue of inheritance to the court system.*

*The women of Nepal are involved in a long-term struggle to gain inheritance rights, which have traditionally been denied them. One element of their strategy has been to use the Convention on the Elimination of All Forms of Discrimination against Women (CEDAW) to highlight the discriminatory nature of the current socio-legal structure. In doing so, women are calling into question a deeply-rooted cultural norm against women owning property in their own right. Groups opposed to women's inheritance rights have attempted to portray women seeking economic equality as driven by greed and a desire to gain economic benefit for themselves. However, women have used the debate to open up discussion in society about the types of ongoing discrimination women of all ages face because of the prevailing patriarchal structure. The effect of deep-seated discrimination and devaluing of women can be observed in such areas as health, education and access to adequate nutrition.*[1]

*Because Nepal is a signatory to CEDAW, the country's laws must not contravene the Convention. However, the court ruling on the case that was filed in 1993 cited concern as to whether the society would be able to adapt to legal changes that would have the effect of altering tradition. The Supreme Court found that the law did discriminate against women, but did not act immediately to invalidate it. Instead, it directed the government to introduce an appropriate bill in parliament, in consultation with women's organizations and other sectors of society. In May 1998, after years of waiting for the inheritance bill to be discussed in parliament, women showed their frustration by organizing a demonstration in which over 100 were arrested.*

NOT ONLY ARE WOMEN IN NEPAL FACING SOCIAL AND CULTURAL bias, but they are being discriminated against by state made laws. For example, inheritance rights are denied to women. To inherit parental property, a daughter has to be thirty-five years old and unmarried. If she does inherit and then marries, she has to return whatever property she inherited from her parents. The justification the government uses is that since she can get a share of her husband's property, there is no discrimination. But even to get a share of her husband's property, a woman has to be thirty-five years old and have been married for fifteen years. And if she fulfills that condition and gets a share of her husband's property, the law allows the husband to bring a second wife without divorcing her.

A divorced woman has only one right, which is to receive maximum alimony for up to five years. If she was the "cause" of the divorce, she is not even given that right. For a widow to be able to inherit a share of her husband's property she must be at least thirty years old. If she is not, she is provided maintenance and the expenses for the religious duties. She has no right to demand the partition of or get a share of her husband's property.

The law in Nepal creates rights on the basis of a woman's marital status, in violation of Article 1 of CEDAW,[2] which guarantees elimination of all forms of discrimination against women. Nepal has already ratified many international instruments, including CEDAW, without any reservations and in Beijing the government committed itself to providing equal inheritance rights to daughters. However, the situation remains at a stand still.

### Violation of Inheritance Rights for Women

Women are considered to be an obligation. They are not considered to be members of the family, and are therefore subject to "giveaway." Child marriage, selective abortion of girls, bigamy and inappropriately matched marriages are all commonly practiced. Women are compelled to live in situations of domestic violence because they are completely dependent on their husbands. Women have no control over resources and little participation in decision-making. Since women are of lower status, their health is in a vulnerable situation. Nepal has one of the highest rates of maternal mortality in the world, and the life expectancy of women is lower than that of men. Since women have no economic rights, there is no expectation or obligation for parents to educate them. Priority is given to the education of sons, so there is a huge gap between men and women in this area. Women are denied equal citizenship rights. A woman is not recognized as an independent personality and not accepted as a family member. This means that a woman is denied the right to transfer citizenship to her own children and spouse.

As second-class citizens, women are dependent on their fathers before marriage, on their husbands during marriage, and in old age on their sons. Existing laws reinforce this system of social values by denying women the right to independently inherit property. The whole situation is not only violating women's human rights, but is also having a negative impact on the overall development of women. This, in turn, impacts on the national development and the national economy.

### Underlying Causes of the Denial of Inheritance Rights for Women

The patriarchal structure; a deeply rooted gender-biased value system; the dominant Hindu religion, which holds that only a son can perform the required religious duties; a lack of recognition of women as independent voters;[3] lack of political will; non-fulfillment of the political manifesto that included an election promise to work for the advancement of women and an end to discrimination; women's lack of power and decision-making; and rampant illiteracy are some of the major causes. In addition to all this, women's economic empowerment is perceived as a threat to society.

### Initiatives Toward Gaining Women's Inheritance Rights

Efforts were made to raise the issue before the public and to amend discriminatory laws through lobbying and advocacy and by efforts to influence law makers and policy makers. When all of those efforts failed, two woman advocates challenged the discriminatory law in the courts,[4] since the new Constitution opened the avenues for public interest litigation. The court declared the existing inheritance provision conditional and gave a directive order to the government to introduce a bill within a year which would require a review of all laws related to property.

How did women's rights activists raise the issue as a human rights issue, and what are the mechanisms under the international instruments used during the process? When the case was filed in the court, CEDAW was referred to as a national law, because under the Treaty Act, which is part of Nepalese law, once any convention is ratified it becomes national law. If there is inconsistency between the existing laws and the Convention, the Convention prevails. This provision encouraged women to use the judicial avenue for seeking inheritance rights.

Similarly, the reporting process available under CEDAW is another mechanism we have for holding the government accountable to its international commitments. When the initial report on CEDAW was submitted by the government of Nepal,[5] we NGOs presented a shadow report[6] where we raised the inheritance issue. In its concluding remarks, the CEDAW Committee said that as a matter of priority, discriminatory laws on property and inheritance rights should be amended. At the same time, the Committee showed its concern that if laws do not conform with culture and tradition, society will be disturbed. This was the concern raised by the Committee members and these concluding comments are being taken very seriously by the Supreme Court of Nepal.

A draft national plan of action to implement CEDAW in the domestic context has already been written, as the CEDAW Committee also stated in its concluding remarks that the government has not taken sufficient action to reflect the convention in domestic policies. However, we feel there are some limitations to working with human rights instruments. For example, non-ratification of the Optional Protocol to CEDAW[7] leaves limited avenues for individuals to use the complaint mechanism at the international level. Also, when we filed the case in the Supreme Court of Nepal, when we referred to Article 15 of CEDAW to guarantee equal inheritance rights for women, the Public Attorney made a strong argument that Article 15 provides for a woman's right to administer property,[8] but does not mention ownership, as is provided for the spouse under Article 16(h).[9]

We feel that people are not much aware of the general recommendations under various articles of CEDAW.[10] The government is not very aware of them either and the concluding comments on various international instruments are not being used effectively. We also feel that NGOs have not been able to mobilize themselves adequately during the preparation and submission of the Shadow Reports under other human rights instruments. We also have been denied access to make our presentation during the reporting on the International Convention on Civil and Political Rights (ICCPR).[11]

We feel that many women's human rights issues have not been able to link up with the broader human rights perspective. Nor have they been able to link up with the various human rights organizations working in the country. Therefore, we feel that there are various challenges. We have to address the issues, including the interpretation of the Court, which on the one hand, criticizes the government for non-compliance and on the other hand takes into consideration the patriarchal values and social structure and the fear of positive discrimination against men. We also feel that there are other challenges, like social instability, lack of gender sensitization and lack of understanding by people in government about the obligations with regard to various international instruments. These are some of the challenges we've been facing.

Despite the various weaknesses and shortcomings, the challenges have had a positive impact on the empowerment of women in the country. Because of the intervention by women activists, the entire society was challenged to start rethinking the patriarchal structure and the status of the individual freedom of women. Women have begun to be vigilant about the issue and link it to the broader issue of equality, forcing the government to reconsider its understanding of equality. And women have become part of the law reform process. The advocacy work has united women and NGOs to continue working for the advancement of women's human rights. As a result of the judicial intervention, the government had to submit a bill in Parliament, which acknowledged in its preamble that its objective was to amend the existing discriminatory laws, as per the Court decision, since Nepal is a party to CEDAW.

However, we feel that there are various strategies which we have to adopt in order to achieve our goal. Some of them are: a media campaign; media monitoring; developing a network from the grassroots to the international level and to international forums like this one; advocacy work toward fulfillment of state obligations; lobbying the government, Parliament, and political parties to pass the bill for monitoring the implementation of national and international commitments; and advocacy towards ratifying the Optional Protocol to CEDAW.

If these strategies fail, we have to prepare to launch a complaint to the Human Rights Committee under the Optional Protocol to the International Convention on Civil and Political Rights (ICCPR), of which Nepal is a party. Finally, we the women of Nepal need your support and attention to get this bill passed and registered in Parliament. It is now just beginning to pass through the Parliamentary system.

# Notes

1. Fewer women than men are enrolled in school and the drop-out rate for women rate is higher. The literacy rate for women is 33 percent compared to 66 percent for men. The maternal mortality rate is high (539 per 100,000 births) and more girls die in infancy and childhood. Women lack access to paid employment and have low participation in public life and government. Sapana Pradhan Malla, *Use of CEDAW in Women's Inheritance Right* (unpublished report, June 2000):2.

2. CEDAW is the abbreviation commonly used to refer to the Convention on the Elimination of All Forms of Discrimination against Women, sometimes called the Women's Convention. The Convention entered into force on September 3, 1981. Article 1 states: "For the purposes of the present Convention, the term 'discrimination against women' shall mean any distinction, exclusion or restriction made on the basis of sex which has the effect or purpose of impairing or nullifying the recognition, enjoyment or exercise by women, irrespective of their marital status, on a basis of equality of men and women, of human rights and fundamental freedoms in the political, economic, social, cultural, civil or any other field."

3. While Nepalese women do have the right to vote, their vote is often manipulated by male family members. According to Sapana Pradhan Malla, this fact is reflected in political posters, which focus on men as the voting base (Personal communication, December 2000).

4. *Dhungana v. Nepal*, Supreme Court of Nepal, Writ No. 3392 of 1993, August 2, 1994, unreported.

5. When a state ratifies CEDAW, it undertakes the obligation to present reports at the United Nations on the progress it has made implementing women's human rights. The first report is due one year after ratification, and a further report is required every four years following that date. These reports are made to the CEDAW Committee, which provides commentary to the Government on actions it should be taking to better implement the Convention. Ilana Landsberg-Lewis (ed.), *Bringing Equality Home: Implementing the Convention on the Elimination of All Forms of Discrimination against Women,* (New York: UNIFEM, 1998):35.

6. While women's NGOs are not formally included in the CEDAW Committee sessions for monitoring compliance with the CEDAW Convention, they are encouraged by the Committee to provide information about where they feel improvement should be made. For this purpose, NGOs have joined together in coalitions to prepare "shadow reports," which describe the state of women's human rights in their countries while commenting on their Government's reports. ibid.

7. The Optional Protocol to CEDAW is an additional formal instrument, separate from the CEDAW convention, that introduces a procedure whereby the Committee on the Elimination of Discrimination Against Women (called the CEDAW Committee) can receive and investigate complaints of cases of discrimination against women, including those brought forth by individuals. However, this option is only available in countries that have ratified both CEDAW and the Optional Protocol.

8. Article 15(2) of CEDAW reads: "States Parties shall accord to women, in civil matters, a legal capacity identical to that of men and the same opportunities to exercise that capacity. In particular, they shall give women equal rights to conclude contracts and to administer property and shall treat them equally in all stages of procedure in courts and tribunals."

9. Article 16(h) of CEDAW reads: "The same rights for both spouses in respect of the ownership, acquisition, management, administration, enjoyment and disposition of property, whether free of charge or for a valuable consideration."

10. The CEDAW Committee interprets the Women's Convention in relation to specific topics by issuing General Recommendations. The General Recommendations on the different articles of CEDAW reflect ongoing and evolving thinking about the Convention, enabling it to be relevant to circumstances that were not anticipated when the document was drafted.

11. The International Covenant on Civil and Political Rights (ICCPR) is one of the six core treaties of the international human rights system. It was adopted by the United Nations on December 16, 1966 and entered into force on March 23, 1976. The Optional Protocol to the ICCPR permits states that have signed it to hear complaints from individuals.

# African Women Refugees in the United Kingdom: Organizing Against Oppression

Sarah Mukasa

*Sarah Mukasa is United Kingdom Program Manager for Akina Mama wa Afrika (AMwA), an international development NGO for African women in Europe and Africa. She is a trainer, feminist activist and campaigner with a special interest in the human rights of refugee and asylum seekers and sexual and reproductive health rights.*

*Akina Mama was set up in 1985 by women from different parts of Africa living in the United Kingdom. Translated from Swahili, the name means "solidarity among African women." The organization was founded to create a space for African women to organize autonomously, identify issues of concern and speak for themselves.*

*Many African women now live in Britain as a result of economic and political crises in their countries. The majority arrive as refugee and asylum seekers or migrants and are often single heads of households. Recent major changes in British government policies with regard to refugees have grave implications for the mental health and physical well being of refugees and migrants. Women with young children are in an especially vulnerable position.*

IT IS A GREAT HONOR AND PRIVILEGE FOR ME TO BE HERE TODAY TO share the stories of refugee women from Africa based in the United Kingdom, who have experienced some of the worst forms of human rights abuses in their countries of origin and who continue to grapple with a largely hostile and unwelcoming environment in the U.K.

These women have faced this adversity with a great deal of courage, dignity and determination. In the midst of all the problems they have in the U.K. trying to deal with basic survival issues, they have organized themselves to provide support, assistance, advice and information to others in the same predicament. Women such as Azah, a refugee from Sudan, who within nine months of arriving in the U.K. as a refugee, had set up an organization to support peace building and reconciliation between northern and southern Sudan. Or the woman from Rwanda, who for the purpose of this presentation I will call Chantal. She has requested that I keep her identity anonymous, as she is worried about the effect it may have on her asylum application. Chantal has joined forces with a group of women from Sierra Leone to set up an organization that will document the human rights abuses of children in these parts of the world.

I should point out that these women ought to have been here to tell their own stories. However, such is the nature of the immigration and asylum laws in the U.K. that those whose asylum applications are being considered by the authorities have severe restrictions on their movements outside of the U.K. The backlog in decision-making on applications by the home office—that is the authority responsible for these decisions—has meant that several asylum seekers have been stranded in the U.K. for up to ten years. Therefore, in the absence of my two colleagues, you will have to make do with me.

Since AMwA was established in 1985, the U.K. programs have, among other things, provided support and advocacy services for refugee women from Africa in the U.K. In 1998, Akina Mama developed capacity-building projects for African women's organizations in the U.K. This project aims to provide organizational development, training and support for community based organizations that do not have access to mainstream services. It is through the provision of these services that we have come into contact with women such as Azah and Chantal.

## Harsh Rules for Asylum Seekers

Before I proceed, I would like to give a contextual framework within which we can assess the achievements of these remarkable women. These are very difficult times for asylum seekers in the U.K. The insidious belief that asylum seekers, especially those from the South, come to the U.K. purely for a better form of life forms the backbone of all current laws on immigration and asylum seeking. Coupled with the widely held belief that those from racial or ethnic minority communities are unskilled and uneducated and are therefore a burden to the U.K. taxpayers, the laws are designed to make entry into the U.K. as difficult as possible for asylum seekers. The phrase "guilty until proven innocent" comes to mind at this point, because asylum seekers have an almost impossible battle to prove that they have a genuine case under the terms of the 1951 UN Convention Relating to the Status of Refugees.[1]

In 1999, the U.K. parliament passed the Immigration and Asylum Act. In it there are a number of elements that many of us working in this field are deeply concerned about. The first is that from April of this year (2000), asylum seekers can be involuntarily dispersed across the country. Those who refused to move to their allocated area lost whatever entitlement they may have to assistance from public funds.

Asylum seekers are often moved to areas they are not familiar with and in which there are no support mechanisms in terms of family, friends and community. The adverse effect that this has, particularly on women and children, is often ignored. A number have found themselves in areas of huge economic and social deprivation and exclusion. In this climate, they have been greeted with a great deal of hostility and suspicion by local residents, with many experiencing frequent racial attacks and abuse. Women and children are especially vulnerable to these attacks.

In addition to the dispersal, the government continued to use the rules on in-country applications for asylum, which required those applying for asylum, once they are in the U.K., to do so within four days of their arrival in the country. Those who apply after this period do not have any recourse to public funds whatsoever, nor are they allowed to work while their applications are being considered by the authorities. As I speak to you now, there are a number of asylum seekers in the U.K. today living in abject poverty—many on the streets, as they have no means of supporting themselves. Voluntary organizations working with refugees are seeing increasing numbers of asylum seekers in these situations and are under enormous strain to provide basic welfare services to them.

## Economic Rights Violated

For those who are lucky enough to get support from public funds, the government operates a voucher system. Instead of cash, asylum seekers are issued vouchers, which they use to purchase essential items such as food and so on. Some shopping areas have allocated times for voucher purchases and also have restrictions on what items can be bought using these vouchers. Asylum seekers have complained that this system makes them vulnerable and open to abuse and harassment from staff and others. This is because they are easily identifiable. Consequently, many asylum seekers, in an effort to make ends meet, find themselves working illegally in dangerous and often exploitative conditions.

Women especially are lured into the sex trade, where they are subjected to violent abuse, not to mention exposure to dangerous and life-threatening infections, such as HIV.

In an effort to speed up the backlog of asylum applications, the government has set up a fast track system and a target of six months for decisions on asylum applications. The main concern here is that the system developed to speed up these decisions denies the asylum seeker due recourse to the process of law, with their losing certain rights to appeal in the case of negative decisions. In addition, the government has continued to use detention centers for asylum seekers who await decision or whose papers are "not in order." This has been a major concern for many of us activists and campaigners. Plans are under way to build more detention centers. Indeed, there's even talk of converting ships at the seaports into detention centers.

Yet, this same government, a year or so ago, revoked the quarantine laws for animals and household pets. Under this law, all household pets entering Britain had to be kept in detention or quarantined for a period of six months in order to control rabies. The government revoked this law on the grounds that it was cruel and inhumane to keep these poor little animals locked up for that period of time. It is in this context that women such as Azah and Chantal, struggling for survival on a day-to-day basis, are striving to organize themselves to be of assistance to others.

## Fleeing Political Persecution

As a student activist, Azah was opposed to the fundamentalist Islamic government's policy on women, and also to the war being waged in southern Sudan. Her outspokenness against the government, and her refusal to comply with government policy on Islamic dress, led to her arrest and subsequent imprisonment without trial. Along with several of her colleagues, many of whom she has neither seen nor heard from again, she was tortured and raped. In addition, the government confiscated her land, and had her under constant surveillance by secret police. She and members of her family were constantly subjected to police harassment and unlawful arrest. She managed to escape to the U.K., where she sought asylum. In the hostel where she was staying, Azah met with other single young women asylum seekers who were struggling to make ends meet. She mobilized them, and in a short space of time they set up a support group and pooled their vouchers together in order to enable them to purchase more goods. Today the support group provides advice and information to young single refugee women on issues such as sexual health and HIV awareness, asylum applications, where to look for bargains, education opportunities, and so on. Azah has also set up an organization whose aim is to bring together women from northern and southern Sudan to build peace and reconciliation. Through the making and selling of traditional crafts, Azah has managed to raise money to send seeds, educational material, bandages and other such items to the war-torn areas of southern Sudan. This she has managed to achieve in the face of her own personal difficulties and challenges.

**Inhumane Rules**
The second sister I wish to speak to you about is Chantal. Chantal is from the Tutsi ethnic group in Rwanda. Chantal lost several members of her family in the genocide, including her husband, parents, sisters and countless members of her extended family. Until a year ago, she did not know the whereabouts of her children, or even if they were alive. With the help of the Red Cross, she managed to track down four of her six children. Her efforts to reunite with her children by bringing them to the U.K. have been met with the stunning and chilling response from the authorities that under the rules, she has to wait for four years before she can bring them to the U.K.

"Sometimes I feel like I'm going to give up," Chantal says. But she has not given up. In fact, she has done the opposite. She has joined forces with a number of women from other war-torn regions in Africa to set up an organization that will campaign for the human rights of children and to document the human rights abuses. One of the aims of the organization is to lobby governments that sell arms to countries that use child soldiers because, in Chantal's own words, "These people are the real criminals. To sell arms in this way is not right, and we must stop it."

**Conclusions**
In conclusion, I will make a few recommendations. The work that many people such as Azah and Chantal do goes largely unrecognized and unsupported. The overwhelming belief, as I stated earlier, is that the vast majority of refugees either have nothing to offer or are poor helpless victims who cannot do anything for themselves. This attitude has to be stopped and the contributions that they make to their communities and to the societies as a whole must be recognized and must be highlighted by the governments and used to educate and influence public opinion. Secondly, there must be gender analysis on the impact of current immigration and asylum legislation. Currently, the vast majority of

gender analysis work is done within the narrow confines of equal opportunities. This is clearly not enough, as it excludes many other areas in which gender discrimination takes place. My final recommendation is that the legislation has to be regarded in the context of institutional racism. The U.K. Government, to its credit, has recognized that it has weaknesses in this area and has taken steps to address them. However, this has not extended to the immigration and asylum legislation or all the government machineries that deal with these issues.

# Note

1. The Convention Relating to the Status of Refugees was adopted in 1951 by the UN Gathering of Plenipotentiaries on the Status of Refugees and Stateless Persons. It entered into force in 1954. The Convention, together with its Protocol (which is an independent, though integrally related, international treaty), are the most comprehensive instruments governing the legal status of refugees which have been adopted at the international level.

# Labor Rights with a Feminist Perspective: Organizing with Workers in the Central American Maquila Industry

*Olga Rivas*

*Olga Rivas has been Executive Director of GRUFE-PROMEFAM, a Guatemalan women's organization that works with poor women in Guatemala City. GRUFE organizes with women who work in the export processing factories, commonly called* maquilas. *Under the maquila system, workers—the majority of which are women—receive low wages and work long hours, usually at piecework rates. Since first being introduced on the Mexico-U.S. border in the mid-1960s, the maquila industry, which specializes in assembling electronic parts and name-brand garments, has been characterized by low wages and poor working conditions. Maquila owners, many of which are transnational corporations, set up factories in countries where wages are low and high unemployment keeps workers from demanding better conditions. Maquilas in Central America have had some of the most abusive working conditions in the hemisphere, including verbal and physical abuse of workers and forced overtime.*

*In 1996, women's rights organizations from Nicaragua, Guatemala, El Salvador and Honduras met in El Salvador to form the Network of Central American Women in Solidarity with Maquila Workers. The network decided that a Code of Ethics was needed to place responsibility on owners for their behavior towards workers and to sensitize governments, the industry, and the public on the need to improve labor practices in the maquilas. The Nicaraguan network member, the María Elena Cuadra Movement of Working and Unemployed Women (MEC) campaigned successfully to have the Code accepted by the*

Nicaraguan Congress. It has been signed into law in that country and endorsed by all the employers of the maquila zone. The MEC trains women workers to monitor the implementation of the Code in the their factories.

Although the other countries participating in the network have not succeeded in having a Code of Ethics adopted, each organization is making progress locally in educating women about their human rights and providing them with skills and training so that they can better protect themselves. GRUFE and the other network groups lobby the ministries of labor in their respective countries and provide advocacy, counseling and accompaniment to workers when abuses occur. They also provide women with literacy training, access to information about health and reproductive rights and weekend workshops on topics that interest them. Network representatives meet regularly to upgrade their skills and receive training in human rights, gender analysis and organizing. They recognize that new and creative types of organizing are necessary in order to support maquila workers in gaining their rights.

I AM GLAD TO HAVE THIS OPPORTUNITY TO SHARE INFORMATION WITH you about the experience of setting up the Central American Network in Solidarity with Maquila Workers—the Red Centroamericana de Mujeres en Solidaridad con las Trabajadoras de la Maquila.

Prior to starting the network, women in the different Central American countries had spent several years gathering and analyzing information about the working conditions and the human rights situation in the transnational assembly plants of Central America, which are commonly referred to as maquila factories. The majority of maquila workers are women. They work under exploitative conditions and frequently experience discrimination. The working conditions are unhealthy and the women are often subjected to violence with regard to their sexual and reproductive rights. The factories may be under national or multinational ownership, but this makes little difference in the treatment of workers. Women who work in the maquilas frequently experience sexual, psychic, physical and verbal violence and most particularly, sexual harassment. One of the greatest ongoing problems workers face is the restriction of freedom of association—which means they are not permitted to form a union in order to protect their rights.

## Setting Up the Network

A few years ago, some Central American women's organizations—some of which refer to themselves as feminist while others do not—began to take on the cause of the maquila workers. In Nicaragua, the María Elena Cuadra Women's Movement (MEC), under the direction of Sandra Ramos; the Coordinating Group of Women's Organizations of El Salvador, led by Isabel Ramírez; the Honduran Women's Collective, led by María Luisa Regalado, and myself, as the representative from Guatemala, convened a meeting of activists who are concerned about the working conditions and the lack of respect for the dignity of maquila workers. The purpose of the meeting was to create a regional organization where we could work together at the national and regional levels to try to develop alternative proposals for confronting the problems maquila workers experience while trying to improve working conditions.

In September 1998, we held a meeting in El Salvador, where we drafted and signed a founding constitution for the network. This was an important step in our process. The objectives of the organization are:

1. to develop and strengthen the network;
2. to work to link other sectors in solidarity with the maquila workers;
3. to influence the design and implementation of government and company policy toward the maquila at the national and international levels.

Since the network began, we have linked women's rights with labor rights, working from a feminist perspective. As a result of efforts in each of our countries, more workers have joined the local organizations and the network has expanded its field of action. We have increased our contact with governments and industry owners and we are working to educate the public about the problems workers face in the maquila. The network's two-pronged approach has permitted us to work to improve the conditions women face in the factories and because of their place in society. In order to do this, we launched a regional campaign to make people aware of the social and labor conditions and the human rights violations the maquila workers experience. Our slogan is "Jobs, yes! But with dignity!"

## Developing a Code of Ethics

The network has developed a Code of Ethics for the maquila industry, one of the main points of which is that it prohibits discrimination against workers who become pregnant. It also prohibits discrimination on the basis of race, religion, age, disability, sexual orientation or political affiliation. The Code contains provisions to ensure that pregnant women can have their jobs back after they give birth, and that they must not be subject to harassment or restriction of their labor rights. The Code states that workers must be treated with respect and dignity and must not be subjected to physical, psychic, sexual or verbal violence. It also states that employers must provide social benefits for underage workers and that workers must receive the legal hourly wage for overtime.

The moral force of the Code is undeniable. Because it is based on women's human rights and labor rights it has become a platform for the demands of maquila workers. By signing the Code, employers and the government commit themselves to respecting and seeking compliance with the human and labor rights of workers.

To date, one of the biggest successes has been the collection by the Nicaraguan group of 30,000 signatures in support of the Code of Ethics. This was due to the work they did to promote the Code with the public. The Nicaraguan women also succeeded in getting the Ministry of Labor and the entity responsible for the maquila zone to sign a ministerial resolution supporting the Code of Ethics as a means of promoting respect for existing labor legislation. This achievement was partly due to the persistent efforts of the women, but also because of the specific historical context of Nicaragua, which has experienced a revolutionary process that has permitted an opening up of some political spaces and has achieved a level of political consciousness among the population.

The Collective of Honduran Women (CODEMUH) managed to establish a dialogue with the Association of Maquila Owners in their country in order to resolve some conflicts that were affecting women workers. In this case, the support of the unions that responded to the awareness campaign was very important. Around this time, the Honduran women also submitted a report to the International Labour Organization (ILO) on the situation of the maquila workers.

In the context of the changes currently taking place in Guatemala, the organizations GRUFE-PROMEFAM and Mujeres en Solidaridad have, for the first time, managed to achieve discussions about the Code of Ethics involving workers, the Ministry of Labor and the Owners Association. However, although the signing of the Peace Accords in 1996 created an improved climate for making some types of social demands, the process has been slower then in some countries due to political instability and a legacy of repression toward social movements, especially unions. There has also been a lack of will on the part of owners to permit workers to fully exercise their human rights.

In El Salvador, the organizations managed to carry out an awareness-raising campaign and to formulate some basic proposals. However, resistance has been greater there so the results, so far, have been minimal.

## Lack of Political Will for Change

Although there have been significant achievements and some progress has been made, we are facing many difficulties. The fundamental obstacles lie in the lack of political will on the part of governments and the refusal of the business sectors to adopt a more flexible position because they are afraid of lowering their profits. In taking stock of our successes and the obstacles we face, we have identified several key areas that need to be addressed.

One of the things we want is for the maquila workers' issues to be placed on the agenda of the unions, the popular organizations and, most importantly, the women's movement. We want these organizations to identify with and take up the struggle for maquila workers' rights and we want to form a broader alliance that will include many types of organizations.

We also want to establish relationships with women who work in the communications media in order to design a strategy for getting our message out so that we can inform people and try to influence public opinion. In doing this, we hope to broaden the possibility for dialogue and reach people and organizations with influence in different areas that may be able to help us reach our objectives.

Finally, it is important to create mechanisms for monitoring the commitments governments of the region have made in which they have said they will respect existing labor laws and respect women's human rights and their rights as workers.

# Poverty in the Midst of Prosperity: Organizing for Economic Rights in the United States

Joy Butts

*Joy Butts is a member of the Kensington Welfare Rights Union (KWRU) who has assumed an active roll of leadership among the poor. She has been homeless and a recipient of U.S. government welfare. She is producer and host of "Marching On," a television program that features the work and campaigns of the KWRU. She uses the show to educate her viewers about the effects of economic human rights violations on the poor in the United States.*

*The Kensington Welfare Rights Union is a multiracial organization led by poor and homeless people, which is dedicated to organizing welfare recipients, the homeless, the working poor and all people concerned with economic justice. Its Poor People's Economic Human Rights Campaign is a national effort to raise the issue of poverty as a human rights violation. In 1999, the KWRU filed a case before the Inter-American Commission of the Organization of American States (OAS) holding the U.S. government accountable for economic human rights abuses caused by corporate downsizing, poverty and welfare reform. In 2000, KWRU coordinated the Poor People's World Summit to End Poverty, where representatives of poor people's organizations from many countries discussed strategies for globalizing their struggle and building an international movement to end poverty, led by the poor.*

THE KENSINGTON WELFARE RIGHTS UNION HAD ITS BEGINNINGS IN 1990 when six women came together to address the issues that were impacting poor women in Kensington, North Philadelphia, which by the way, is the poorest district in the state of Pennsylvania. From that beginning, our membership has grown to include poor men, women and children, students and people from all walks of life—locally, nationally and internationally—who are joined with us in organizing to realize our mission statement, which is "Building a movement to end poverty as we know it today."

Over the last several years, the KWRU has been fighting against welfare reform[1] and against increased poverty, and fighting for our economic human rights. We have exhausted all of the official channels at the local, state and national levels. We, the poor, unemployed and homeless people of this country, have marched on city halls, lobbied at state capitals and testified in Washington, D.C., and still our government continues to implement policies like welfare reform, that deny Americans their economic human rights.

On May 16, 1996, the state of Pennsylvania's Governor Tom Ridge signed into law Act 1996-35, otherwise known as the TANF Bill.[2] The provisions of the Act are to:

1. encourage personal and parental responsibility;
2. emphasize self-sufficiency through employment;
3. strengthen child support requirements; and
4. increase penalties for welfare fraud.

## Welfare "Reform" Brings Hardship

I want to make note of the fact that—emphasizing the second point, "self-sufficiency through employment"—two years ago there were 134 unemployment offices in the state of Pennsylvania. As of today, there are eight for the entire state.[3] There are no jobs.[4] The Personal Responsibility and Work Opportunity Reconciliation Act of 1996 is the welfare reform bill that President Clinton signed into law and then made the statement that he was going to fix it—and we're still waiting for him to fix it.[5] The final rules were published in the Federal Register on April 12, 1999. This ended Aid to Families with Dependent Children, known as AFDC, a sixty-year-old federal entitlement program, and also the federal JOBS[6] employment and training program, which means that there no longer is a safety net for women and children in the United States of America.[7]

What was supposed to be a benevolent system has now been transformed into a system in which the poor are being treated like criminals. The TANF Bill, which stands for "temporary assistance to needy families," is a five-year lifetime bill. After your five years are up, you are no longer able to receive welfare benefits. This will take place for some people in 2001.

In this year 2000, the least organized group are poor women around the world. They represent a powerful force. What kind of women's movement is there without the inclusion of poor women? Therefore, KWRU is using organizing tools to facilitate organizing the poor. There is a film clip coming up. It's about the work we do and I'd like to extend an invitation to everyone here. When you're in Philadelphia, Pennsylvania next time, stop by our office. We'll take you on a tour of devastation and poverty in the United States of America, in the City of Brotherly Love.

### Economic Human Rights Campaign

Kensington Welfare Rights Union's mission to build leaders from among the ranks of the poor has taken on many diverse forms. In 1996, we kicked off our Economic Human Rights Campaign with our first "March For Our Lives," which was a 140 mile march from Philadelphia to the state capital in Harrisburg, Pennsylvania, protesting the governor's welfare cuts on the state level. It was in the middle of winter and some of us almost froze to death on the steps of the capital. In 1997, after the passage of the national welfare reform law, we began to take our case before the world, with the March For Our Lives, number two, from the Liberty Bell in Philadelphia—so called, the cradle of liberty—to the United Nations in New York City. In June 1998, we led the New Freedom Bus Tour around the United States—thirty-five stops, collecting documentation of economic human rights violations, using Articles 23, 25 and 26 of the Universal Declaration of Human Rights[8] to demand freedom from unemployment, hunger and homelessness.

In October 1999, we marched over 400 miles—the March of the Americas—continuing to march for our lives from Washington, D.C. to the UN in New York, joining with our sisters and brothers from the Southern Hemisphere to protest and document the poverty that is increasing in our country and in all parts of this hemisphere. And yes, while we were commemorating the fiftieth anniversary of the Universal Declaration of Human Rights (UDHR), signed by 184 countries at the UN in 1948—including the United States—we have been specifically documenting violations of Articles 23,[9] 25[10] and 26,[11] which guarantee every human being the right to a job at a living wage, the right to organize, the right to affordable housing, the right to medical care and the right to education.

In this country, we have 45 million people—working poor—who have no health insurance. In this country, over half of the homeless are working. We have, in this country, a serious situation because on the six o'clock news we hear about the robust economy. It's broadcast on CNN. It's broadcast on the

BBC around the world, so when we go to Europe to speak they ask us about the robust economy. Well, organizations like KWRU, who don't have access to Madison Avenue advertising, have to do our own form of advertising, and this is one of our forms. We also have a cable show through Drexel University, called *Marching On*, which has been in existence for a year-and-a-half. I was asked by the director to produce and host a show and it was really a challenge because I had never been in front of a camera before that.

### Using the Human Rights System to Defend the Rights of Poor People

Specifically, under the UDHR, Articles 23, 25 and 26 talk about the right to a job and a living wage, which is very important in this country, because the majority of the people who are on welfare and are still receiving it—in most of the larger cities your rent is running you 500 or 600 dollars. If you're getting 400 dollars a month, then you already know that you're behind the eight ball. You haven't included utilities; you haven't included what it takes to buy clothes, for transportation, etc.

I'd like to list some of the affiliates that we have. We are affiliated with the National Union of Hospital and Health Care Employees; the American Federation of State, County, and Municipal Employees; and the AFL-CIO. Over the past few years, we've had to come together and join with other groups in order to get the word out and for people in the U.S.A. and around the world to understand the seriousness of what's going on with poverty in this country. We have had our economic human rights campaigns, we've had human rights schools, where we go around the country and we educate people while we're organizing at the same time, about the fact that they do, indeed, have economic human rights. We have a website: www.kwru.org and we want you to check us every other day, or whenever you get a chance. We have a listserve, which you can join. Right now, at this point, we're preparing for the Republican Convention, which is coming to Philadelphia.

I just want to give you an idea of what's going on. Now, we've had the CIA, the Secret Service, in Philadelphia for the last three months. We've had all of Bush's people in Philadelphia for the last three months. KWRU put in a petition to have a march. We were denied. We were not surprised. We will still have our march on July 31.[12]

### We Will Not Disappear!

We're concerned about something else that is happening in Philadelphia because of this Republican Convention: the fact that they're getting ready to remove all the homeless off the street. This is very serious. A large part of what we do is to win housing for people. Over the past nine years we have won housing for over 450 people. I'm one of the people that they were able to win housing for, and part of the Clintonville Tent City. That is how I and four other members got their housing. And I'm going to explain how that's done because that's very important, I think, for people to understand the strategy we use, since we have no money.

We simply find an empty lot, preferably a city lot. And then we put tents on it. And we put signs up, and we get all the homeless people on the streets that need housing and we put them in there. And sooner or later we get one of the TV stations to come down and ask us what's going on. Now, in between that, we're going to deal with the city and the shelter system and in between that, they're going to probably say, "Okay, okay, okay. We'll get housing for 'x' number of people." But that's just one of the ways that we do it.

To close, what I want to say to all of you is that there is a danger in this country of making the poor invisible, of having them disappear from sight, and so we're saying to all of you: We will continue to have a voice. We will be heard. Thank you.

## Notes

1. In 1996, the Personal Responsibility and Work Opportunity Reconciliation Act (PRWORA) was passed in the United States. This piece of legislation ended the nationally funded programs of economic assistance to poor people, commonly referred to as "Welfare." Breaking with precedents that had been set sixty-one years before, the "reform" transfers responsibility for public assistance from the U.S. Government to the individual states, placing an emphasis on drastically cutting back the number of people who are eligible for welfare. In the months leading up to the legislation's passing, debate in Congress by some of the reform's supporters focused on condemning and criticizing poor people—particularly women of color and single mothers. Although it is presented in terms that promote employment and self-sufficiency, in reality the new legislation destroys an already eroded social safety net, further increasing the vulnerability of the poor during a time of growing economic inequality. The fact that each state essentially sets its own rules has resulted in considerable variance as to how the basic components of the program are applied.

2. The Temporary Assistance for Needy Families (TANF) program and the Personal Responsibility and Work Opportunity Reconciliation Act (PRWORA) are the two components of U.S. welfare reform legislation. They replace the previous national program entitled Aid to Families with Dependent Children (AFDC). Under the TANF program, there is a five-year (60 month) limit on the amount of time a family can receive welfare benefits, after which no more assistance will be

made available. The first people to reach this time limit will do so in 2001. Women who are raising children on their own who apply for TANF must supply information about their children's father, who will then be required to contribute child support payments. It is estimated that one-half of the women who receive economic assistance are fleeing domestic violence (Institute for Food and Development Policy: http://www.foodfirst.org).

3. The function of the state-run unemployment offices is to provide access to Unemployment Insurance—temporary funding for workers who lose their jobs—and to act as employment centers by providing information about job vacancies. According to the KWRU, the decline in the number of offices reflects the fall in job availability along with increasingly restricted access to Unemployment Insurance.

4. A major component of the welfare reform act is that people who receive economic assistance must apply for and accept jobs. The law allows states to create jobs by taking money previously used for welfare checks that went directly to recipients and using it to create community service jobs or to provide hiring incentives for potential employers. Pennsylvania, which was once a manufacturing center, has experienced a high rate of plant closure and corporate downsizing. Globalization and increasing automation in the workplace have resulted in massive job loss. The new rule, which requires welfare recipients to seek jobs, had the effect of flooding the job market so that only 12 percent of the new job seekers found work. At the end of 2000, the unemployment rate in Kensington was 74 percent (Source: KWRU).

5. In a statement released by the White House the day the welfare reform legislation was voted on, President Bill Clinton remarked that while, in general, he was pleased with the legislation, "Some parts of this bill still go too far. And I am determined to see that those areas are corrected." He then expressed concern that cuts to assistance funding would affect the nutrition of poor families: "...I am concerned that although we have made great strides to maintain the national nutritional safety net, this bill still cuts deeper than it should in nutritional assistance, mostly for working families with children." Clinton also expressed disappointment that the Congress had attached a provision denying access to welfare benefits, including health care assistance, to families that had legally immigrated to the United States (*Statement by the President,* July 31, 1996. Available at: http://libertynet.org/~edcivic/welfclin2.html).

6. The Job Opportunity and Basic Skills Training program (JOBS) was a program that provided skills training and help with finding a job to people covered by the Aid to Families with Dependent Children (AFCD) program. Under the JOBS program, participants were permitted to continue receiving economic assistance while undergoing training and for up to one year after being hired for a job. Training under the program was geared to participants' needs and could include basic education or technical courses. It was aimed at helping participants gain the skills needed to apply for better jobs than they would previously have been able to aspire to.

7. People working under the PRWORA program receive wages that are often below minimum wage and few or no benefits. Although they may be performing the same tasks as others in the workplace, they are relegated to a different status from other workers. They have no right to leave a job or complain about working conditions. Not following the guidelines for seeking work or not remaining in a job once placed can cause a family to be eliminated from the program (Alan Weil, "Where is Welfare Reform Heading?" *San Francisco Chronicle,* September 22, 2000).

8. The Universal Declaration of Human Rights (UDHR) is the basic international pronouncement of the fundamental rights of all human beings. It was proclaimed by the United Nations on December 10, 1948 as the "common standard of achievement for all peoples and all nations." It outlines the inalienable rights for all humanity and has set the direction for all further work in the area of human rights.

9. Article 23 of the UDHR covers areas related to work. Section 1 of the article states: "Everyone has the right to work, to free choice of employment, to just and favourable conditions of work and to protection against unemployment. Section 3 of the article states: "Everyone who works has the right to just and favourable remuneration ensuring for himself [sic] and his family an existence worthy of human dignity, and supplemented, if necessary, by other means of social protection."

10. Article 25 of the UDHR states: "Everyone has the right to a standard of living adequate for the health and well-being of himself and of his family, including food, clothing, housing and medical care and necessary social services, and the right to security in the event of unemployment, sickness, disability, widowhood, old age or other lack of livelihood in circumstances beyond his control."

11. Article 26 of the UDHR covers the right to education. It states: "Everyone has the right to education. Education shall be free, at least in the elementary and fundamental states. Elementary education shall be compulsory. Technical and professional education shall be made generally available and higher education shall be equally accessible to all on the basis of merit."

12. Prior to the U.S. Democratic Party Convention, which was held in Philadelphia in July 2000, KWRU followed the standard legal procedure of applying to the city government for a permit to hold a march. It was denied, making KWRU the only group to be denied such a permit during either the Democratic or the Republican conventions that year. KRWU decided to march anyway and did so, without incident, on July 31. The estimated number of participants was 15,000 (http://www.kwru.org).

# Building a Culture of Women's Human Rights in Nigeria

Ayesha Imam

*Ayesha Imam is Executive Director of BAOBAB for Women's Human Rights. She has been a lecturer and researcher in women's studies and gender analysis at universities and research institutes in Nigeria, the U.K., Canada and Senegal. She has also worked on providing gender training to activists in NGOs, and for researchers, government officials and mid-level planners. She has been a women's rights, social justice and democracy advocate since she was in her teens.*

*BAOBAB focuses on women's legal rights under customary, statutory and religious laws in Nigeria. BAOBAB networks with and is part of the international women's rights movement. As part of the Women Living Under Muslim Laws (WLUML) international solidarity network, BAOBAB serves as the coordination office for Africa and the Middle East.*

THE ISSUE FOR US WAS: HOW DO WE GET CHILDREN AND YOUNG people thinking about human rights? How do we ensure that when they do think about human rights, that it is in a way that integrates women's human rights? And how do we begin building a human rights culture—a women's human rights culture—under a military regime and after decades of military rule? These are the questions we were asking ourselves.

## A Culture of Rights Violations

Nigeria is the most populous nation in Africa. Until May 1999, Nigeria had been under military rule for the past sixteen years. In fact, Nigeria has been ruled by military regimes since 1966, with the exception of a brief period of four years between 1979 and 1983. Thus, any Nigerian under sixteen has never lived under anything except military and despotic rule. Anybody under thirty has lived similarly in all but four years of their life—between the ages of nine and thirteen or younger—which they may just remember, but they are unlikely to have been active participants in a civilian regime. And you must remember that, like many countries in Africa, Asia, and Latin America, in Nigeria the majority of the population is young.

Since 1984, and particularly in the last couple of years, the military has been more and more arbitrary and despotic and violating of human rights. Arbitrary arrests, detention without trial, armed forces presence on the streets—including daily harassment of passersby and motorists—have been the norm. They've been part of everyday experience. So a culture of toleration of violence from the state—but also from civil society—has grown up together with a very cynical and pessimistic attitude towards human rights assertions. Even if you know what rights exist in theory, you don't believe that you're ever going to be able to actually exercise them.

In particular, there are, and continue to be flagrant violations of women's human rights, despite the ratification of CEDAW in 1985 and despite Nigeria's participation in the Decade for Women conferences in Nairobi and Beijing—all of which happened under military rule. There continues to be an exclusion of women from power and decision-making, except as appendages of men, which is a feature we call in Africa the "First Lady syndrome."

Of course, this is not surprising, given that the military is, almost by definition, a male dominant, male-bonded institution, and it necessarily reinforces these values as well as being an authoritarian and top-down culture that regards all civilians—but especially women—as incapable. So the state values in Nigeria over the past thirty years have reinforced and strengthened those values and discourses in Nigerian cultures which already accept the male as the norm, accept male preference, and accept the idea of women and girls as lower in status and power.

In the past few years, especially, there has been a great deal of human rights activism in Nigeria protesting the violations by the state of civil and political rights. This helped in the restoration of civilian rule last year, and is continuing to help in the movement towards actual democracy as opposed to merely civilian rule. However, by and large, the mainstream human rights movements in Nigeria have accepted the "male as norm" culture, and they focus on violations by the state which mostly, although not solely, affect men directly.

However, violations of women's rights are carried out not only by the state, but also by other actors in civil society. Often violations of women's rights are not only in the pubic domain but even more frequently in the private domain. But this is not being recognized, so that, for example, the right to peace and security—Article 2 of the Universal Declaration of Human Rights[1]— is frequently understood in Nigerian mainstream human rights practice as concerning freedom from state violations, like arbitrary arrests and detentions or armed forces in custodial violence. But it has not been seen to include the right of women not to be beaten up by husbands, by partners or by other members of their households. And this is despite the fact that actually far more people are injured, hospitalized or murdered by domestic violence than by the state in arbitrary arrests and custodial violence, even at the height of the worst excesses of the military regime in Nigeria.

Thus, not only has the experience of children and young people been of rights violations, but the mainstream human rights activism that they have seen has not been gender aware in its conceptualization and practice. And that is what we at BAOBAB for Women's Human Rights started with—with the idea that it was necessary to extend human rights thinking and activism so that it takes into account those violations that mostly affect women, as well as those that mostly affect men, and that furthermore, we need to bring in younger generations to a wider and more inclusive view of human rights.

## A Poster Competition

In 1998, while we were still under military rule, during a series of elections that previously in Nigeria were a little bit like mirages—they moved further and further away as you got nearer to the horizon—we decided to undertake a project with three aims. We sought to intervene in raising issues of human rights among young people and to start talking and thinking about rights in a way that they would take for granted that women's rights are part of the discourse of human rights. Second, we wanted them to focus on what are women's human rights in terms of everyday experiences, rather than charters and government documents. Third, we sought to find a way so that children and young people would start recognizing violations of women's human rights in their own experience, in their own daily lives.

So what did we do? Well, we held a competition to design a poster on the theme "Building a Women's Human Rights Culture in Nigeria." There were three age categories—children up to twelve years; teenagers thirteen to nineteen; and young adults, twenty to thirty. And so we produced a series of handbills and posters giving information about the competition and distributed them to NGOs in Nigeria.

Our organization, BAOBAB, collaborates with and runs an information service for around 250 NGOs that deal with women's rights and human rights issues in Nigeria. So we turned to this network as well as to our own state outreach teams—of which we have thirteen—to help distribute the information about the competition to schools, youth clubs and youth projects. We also distributed on request copies of the Universal Declaration of Human Rights and the African Charter for Human and Peoples' Rights, which is important because it is the only one that has actually been domesticated in Nigeria.[2] And we distributed CEDAW—the Convention on the Elimination of All Forms of Discrimination against Women.[3]

We received hundreds of entries, which showed the different understandings of youth about women's rights issues. The selection process took place in October 1998, and prizes were awarded to the successful contestants at a ceremony at the National Museum in December. Of course, that date was deliberately chosen to be part of the 16 Days of Activism Against Gender Violence[4] and also because it was close to December 10.[5]

## Building Awareness of Women's Human Rights

What were the effects of this? I think it was fairly clear that the process of making children and young people aware of women's human rights has certainly been strengthened and been infused by this project. For instance, there were, obviously, the hundreds of entries that we got from the children who participated. But more than that, there were the teachers and youth leaders who as a result, got asked questions in their classes such as, "What are human rights? What does it mean?" And sometimes they turned to us or other human rights and women's rights groups to come and facilitate discussion on that issue.

In fact, the effect spread far beyond the children who actually sent in entries. First of all, there was an exhibition of sixty-four of the best entries at the National Museum in Lagos, which is still a very popular place for schools to take children, so it influenced a lot of the children in the Lagos area itself. Secondly, the exhibition also moved to other places. The curator of the National Museum started out being very wary. They didn't want us to hold the exhibition there at all to start with, but then she came down and looked at the entries and was so charmed by them that she volunteered that we should be able to send it to venues of the National Museum in other cities, apart from Lagos. Other NGOs in Nigeria took it to various other cities. Yet other groups used it in Lagos. The Center for Women and Adolescent Empowerment in Yola wants to borrow it. So the exhibition's been going around.

In addition, fourteen of the entries were actually printed as posters and those were distributed very widely to other groups and also, of course, back to the children and the schools where the entries came from so that they felt a sense of ownership of what had been produced. These posters go on being used during the workshops of BAOBAB and other NGOs across Nigeria. For example, during the CEDAW Coalition,[6] quite often one of the posters is used so that the posters not only support consciousness raising, but also are tools in part of the campaign for legal change and advocacy within Nigeria.

We have used the poster designs—twelve of them—on a calendar for the year 2000, which is also distributed free and is very popular. We keep getting requests to get more "because somebody has taken it off my desk because they liked it so much." Other groups are also copying the idea of having a talent hunt and influencing children, which means that they also thought it was a successful thing to do. In addition, children, teachers and youth project leaders have constantly been contacting us and saying, "Can we have another competition?" And this time can *their* schools and *their* youth projects be included?

The media have been asking us for more information about it and writing stories about it. That is an important issue in Nigeria, in which there are accusations that the media do things only on receipt of "brown envelopes" (bribes) and especially only publish stories about women's rights if they're paid to do so. In this case, the project has helped to encourage media to feature women's human rights approvingly, rather than in caricature, which is the usual case. And again, we think that is an important aid to building women's human rights in Nigeria.

## Expanding the Project

So we're doing it again this year. This year we've extended it to not only art but also to writing and music, and we're doing it in collaboration with Jazz 58, which is a youth group which focuses on youth rights in Nigeria. You can see that actually, the poster that we put out is rather boring. The entries that we get are *much* more imaginative.

So what have we learned? First of all, that children are not so unaware of rights as has been assumed. Second, that the highest number of entries was from areas where we did follow-up with the adults who work with those children. Third, that boys' participation in the competition was very high. In fact, it was more than half and this surprised us a lot. When we thought about it, of course, what we realized was that boys have more access to schooling than girls do, so projects that are targeted at schools will reach boys more often than they reach girls. But what's very heartwarming for those of us who are mothers of sons, is that it shows that boys are not born little chauvinists.

A fourth thing we learned is that the issues were clear regardless of religious and cultural diversities of the children. Nigeria is very religiously and culturally diverse, but the issues they picked up on were remarkably similar and the ways in which they thought about them were remarkably similar. They were, for example, very aware of the multiple and interlocking nature of violations of women's rights, and lots of the posters were like this one, which is called "It's an Abuse," showing two or three different things happening.

Violence against women was the biggest single theme, especially of children under thirteen, who are the groups most likely to be drawing on their own experience. So, for us, it supported our contention about the need to take human rights issues off the exclusive focus on the state and into the private arena also.

**Challenges for the Future**

So what are the challenges now? First of all, we need to reach further. We need to reach not only more schools, but in particular to target girls' schools. But even more important than that, we need to target that majority of girls and boys who aren't in school at all. Second, now that BAOBAB and other NGOs have actually been doing work in the area of children's rights—we've been working for example in Kano and Kaduna and in Yola, on early marriage—we are wondering whether the children will start putting those kinds of things in the posters. This would begin to directly challenge men's powers to sexually exploit girls and young women as well as both Muslim and Christian fundamentalists' ideas of morality. That may well provoke a kind of backlash that so far we've been able to avoid.

Finally, this is only an initial step in the process of building a woman's rights culture in Nigeria. As a result of initiatives like this, more and more state institutions, such as the police, as well as the schools, are accepting that there is a need for retraining to raise their own awareness of human rights issues. But we will need to keep pushing to make sure that that conceptualization of human rights issues consciously takes into account the human rights of women.

# Notes

1. The Universal Declaration of Human Rights (UDHR) is the basic international pronouncement of the fundamental rights of all human beings. It was proclaimed by the United Nations on December 10, 1948 as the "common standard of achievement for all peoples and all nations." It outlines the inalienable rights for all humanity and has set the direction for all further work in the area of human rights. Article 2 states that these rights shall be available to all without distinction.

2. The African Charter on Human and Peoples' Rights is also known as the Banjul Charter on Human and Peoples' Rights. Its text was approved at Banjul, Gambia in January 1981. Before international treaties can give rise to legal claims in Nigeria, they have to be "domesticated" i.e. formally adopted by the legislature or, in authoritarian regimes, by the military.

3. The Convention on the Elimination of All Forms of Discrimination against Women, frequently referred to as CEDAW or the Women's Convention, entered into force on September 3, 1981. Monitoring for compliance with CEDAW is carried out by the Committee for the Elimination of Discrimination Against Women. Governments are expected to report periodically to the Committee on progress made and impediments faced toward ending discrimination against women. Nigeria signed and ratified CEDAW in 1985. However, it has not yet been domesticated.

4. The 16 Days of Activism Against Gender Violence is an international campaign that takes place each year between November 25 and December 10. Since its beginning in 1991, individuals and groups around the world have used this 16-day period to create a solidarity movement which raises awareness about gender-based violence, works to ensure better protection for survivors of violence and calls for its elimination. For information about the 16 Days, see the Center for Women's Global Leadership's website: http://www.cwgl.rutgers.edu/.

5. December 10,1998—the year of the first BAOBAB poster competition—was the 50th anniversary of the UDHR.

6. In 1998, a national network of Nigerian women's NGOs described their government's report to the CEDAW Committee as "inaccurate" in its positive portrayal of the status of women. The NGO CEDAW Coalition issued an alternative or "shadow" report that was critical of the government's failure to remove impediments and social discrimination faced by women. The report was used by the CEDAW Committee of the UN to raise questions and make recommendations to the Nigerian government. In Nigeria, the CEDAW Coalition continues to use the shadow report to raise consciousness about women's rights and situation, and to press for the domestication and implementation of CEDAW.

# Breakthrough—Using Popular Culture to Raise Social Awareness

*Mallika Dutt*

BREAKTHROUGH IS AN ORGANIZATION COMMITTED TO INCREASING public dialogue and awareness about human rights and social justice through the use of education and popular culture. Based in India, with offices in Delhi and New York, the group works to create a dialogue that it hopes will catalyze greater community involvement in finding solutions to common problems. Breakthrough brings together creative people working in a variety of art forms. Its goal is to create music, art and television for social change. Its mission is to promote the message of women's rights in India.

Breakthrough was conceived and founded by Mallika Dutt, a human rights activist and lawyer with a history of social involvement. Dutt worked for a number of years in the United States, where she founded Sakhi, a group which addresses violence against women living in the Indian community in New York. She left her job as a human rights program officer for the Ford Foundation to promote Breakthrough full time. Mallika Dutt spoke of Breakthrough's work at the Women 2000 Symposium, and a video showing the making of the group's cd was screened, providing a look at other paths human rights activists are taking in order to make a difference.

Breakthrough's first project—a music recording—has been met with success. Titled *Mann ke Manjeere*, "An Album of Women's Dreams," it focuses on raising awareness about human rights and women's issues. In the words of Mallika Dutt: "The music and the songs describe the lives and hopes of millions of women around the country."

*Manjeere* brought together composers, lyricists, musicians, singers and video artists to produce a high-quality recording that carries a message of women's empowerment. All of the singers are women, working in a variety of folk, classical and pop styles. They are accompanied by innovative musical arrangements that appeal to a range of listeners. The recording has received public acclaim and has been written about and represented in television, print and radio. It is accompanied by a widely-shown music video, which won the prestigious Videocon Screen Awards for Best Music Video of 2000.

Breakthrough uses its web page to link readers to information about social and human rights issues in India, including domestic violence, education for girls and women, and the need for women and men to share housework equally. The web page includes suggestions about ways to get involved in working for social change.

"If we can reach people through this medium," says Dutt, "and share women's hopes, dreams and feelings through the music, then perhaps we can get people to support them. India has one of the highest rates of violence against women in the world today. If we are to really be part of the new century, then we must recognize the contribution of half the country's population. By enabling women, instead of discriminating against them, we can unleash a whole new energy in the development process. That would be a real breakthrough."

Breakthrough's website can be found at: http://www.letsbreakthrough.org.

COMMENTARY
# Holding Both States and the Private Sector Accountable

*Pierre Sané*

I REMEMBER FIVE YEARS AGO IN BEIJING WE HAD A SIMILAR SESSION that was organized by the Center for Women's Global Leadership. The room was full, in spite of all the efforts by the Chinese government to prevent us, as NGOs, from exchanging freely. But when I looked at the room, and given the issues that we were discussing—protection of women's rights, advancing the human rights of women—I just regretted that we did not have the chiefs of staff of the different armies of the world, the chiefs of police of the different countries, and the chief executive officers of multinational corporations, ministers of interiors, and such. Those are the ones who really need to be educated more than the children, as Ayesha Imam has shown earlier.

## Women: A Local and Global Force for Change

I think maybe we can see three very brief lessons from the presentations we have heard. First of all, that women have become a local and a global force for change, and they won't go away. Secondly, the innovative practices to bring international standards to local realities, and we have heard that they are taking place everywhere. It is not just in the South, but in the United States, in the U.K., in Nepal, in Guatemala. So a forum like this, which allows this exchange of experience, will allow women's organizations and human rights organizations to continue to be the force for change that we are all looking for. Thirdly, the rights of women have advanced despite the governments, and I repeat what

Asma Jahangir said earlier: Governments owe us a debt. We want it paid with interest. We do not want it restructured to our disadvantage.

Over the next week, the governments will be discussing that debt and there is a great risk that they will restructure it to the disadvantage of women, so we will have to be extremely vigilant.

We have heard very interesting cases described. The case in Nepal of how the women's organizations have used the courts to direct the government to address legislation and make sure it will be in conformity with the treaties that the government has ratified also shows the need to educate government officials, parliamentarians and judges on the implications of the treaties that their governments ratify. Even governments who are favorable to international human rights law need to be educated. As Martin Luther King Jr. said, the shallow understanding of people of good will is more frustrating than the total misunderstanding of people of ill will. So, we need to educate even those who are of good will so that they understand that ratifying the treaty goes beyond just putting a signature on a piece of paper and therefore being a member of the gang of the good guys.

In terms of innovations, I think the story we heard from Akina Mama in the U.K. shows that innovation and contribution can come from women in different and difficult circumstances. It is not just formal women's organizations or human rights organizations, but the story of these individual refugees in a hostile environment in the U.K.—that is very hostile for asylum seekers and refugees—who are still devoted to and engaged in peace and reconciliation processes and human rights protection in Africa. We need to recognize and support those initiatives and initiatives coming from poor women. We heard the example of taking action in the case of Kensington Welfare Rights Union, from the city halls, state capitals, federal capital, and the mobilizing of world opinion. So political mobilization is extremely important because it is through mobilization that we will ensure that the laws—the good laws—are implemented.

### Forcing Recognition of Corporate Responsibility for Human Rights

Another innovative approach is pushing for the development of codes of ethics. And we have found, working with multinational corporations, that actually companies are willing to develop those codes of conduct—and many multinational corporations now have glossy magazines which describe their commitment to international human rights, and so on. That's the first step. We want to develop them and many are skeptical about the exercise. But, I think it's important as a first step because it allows us to force them to recognize that they have certain responsibilities when it comes to protection of human rights. And the second step is to force them to implement these codes and expose them when they are failing to implement them—expose the hypocrisy and hit them at the bottom line—which is profit. I think the work that is being done in Guatemala for the women assembly workers will progress once we build the alliances, reaching out to the trade unions, and strengthening the monitoring mechanisms on labor rights, especially.

On human rights education—especially when it comes to the rights of women—the initiative in Nigeria shared with us today has taught us that we have to start from the reality of women's lives and not develop education about women's rights starting from a state-centric approach to human rights. And we see here again that children may be more aware of the issues, the realities, and be, therefore, more open to addressing these violations than many in official positions who have the power to address them.

COMMENTARY
# Making the Connections: Using Women's Experiences to Link Human Rights Issues

Sunila Abeyesekera

I AM GOING TO TRY TO LOOK AT A FEW THINGS THAT WERE PRESENT IN all the presentations that we heard during this afternoon. Some of the issues that women from across the globe were talking about are indeed issues about which governments do not seem so convinced at this moment when they are negotiating the Outcomes Document for the Beijing review.

One of the things that has really been exciting about doing women's human rights work has been the possibility, through using women's real experiences, to make the connection between what have traditionally been two separate areas of human rights work—that is, the civil and political rights and the social, economic and cultural rights. As women spoke, whether it was about poverty and unemployment in the United States or about women factory workers or migrant women, you saw how clearly the experience, and the responses and the activism that women create to deal with the injustices that arise out of that experience, make the connection between poverty, economic circumstances, and the social frameworks within which women live. Social and cultural factors affect women's ability to enjoy civil and political rights and live as full citizens, and I think that part of what the women's human rights community has contributed to the human rights discourse has been the reaffirmation of the indivisibility of human rights.

The second point that struck me as I was listening to the testimonies is that women are talking about using legal standards, including international human rights standards, to hold states accountable for their commitments to equality and justice for women. As most of you will see in the coming week, this is a very important piece of what is not being reflected in the Outcomes Document in the UN. Sapana Pradhan Malla from Nepal was talking about how they use the text of the Women's Convention in trying to fight for women's right to equal inheritance. There were many references to labor law, to all kinds of international standards that are not only linked to the Women's Convention but are linked to other very critical pieces of international human rights law, like the Covenant on Civil and Political Rights. Because of the women's human rights movement, I think women across the world have begun to realize that these standards are important and that they create a framework within which we may legitimately claim our rights as women, not only from our governments, but from the international community.

## Women Are Claiming Their Rights

I think this is extremely exciting because, for example, when women have not been able to claim justice within their national systems, through being informed of the global human rights framework they are seeing the possibility of going to the Inter-American Commission, or to the Human Rights Committee which monitors the implementation of the Covenant on Civil and Political Rights, and so forth. Not only are they seeing human rights and women's human rights as being interconnected, but they are seeing the instruments of international human rights as being interconnected. They are seeing that there are many sites within the human rights system where we may legitimately claim our rights. I think that is a really amazing thing to discover because if you had asked me ten years ago what our capacity would be to develop our knowledge of the system and our imagination about how we could use it, up to this point I would have said, "Not much."

I used to have this idea that human rights was the domain of lawyers and for me, one of the most exciting experiences of my activism in women's human rights has been to see women activists learn the law on the run. There are many women activists that I know around the world today who are far more aware of the details of using this system than people who have been to law school for years and who have studied it in books.

## Using Creative Mobilizing Strategies

The third thing that I found interesting about the presentations is that women activists have evolved ways of organizing and mobilizing around human rights issues that is very new, and perhaps challenging to the human rights work that a lot of groups have done before. This type of innovative and creative activism was there, for example, in the Civil Rights movement in the United States, but if you look at human rights work in a lot of our countries, it has largely been focused on legal strategies—filing cases, negotiating with state agencies and so forth. But actually mobilizing women and men to go out on the streets and claim their rights as human rights—not only as workers, not only as migrants, but as human beings saying that just by virtue of being born human, we are entitled to our rights. That has been a very exciting piece of the activism that we have seen women talk about today.

It is also interesting that women have spoken about using the law while being very clearly aware that the law is not the only place from which we can get justice and redress for the injustices that are done to us as women. Women spoke about using education, but they are not only talking about formal education in schools and universities; they are talking about the various non-formal means of education that have been developed by women's groups all over the world. Women talked about using the media, but they are not only talking about the mainstream media; they are talking about creating alternative forms of media for women. And I think the testimonies you have heard today and the multitude of forms of expression which you find displayed on the display tables outside this room are good examples of this creative energy that has transformed human rights forever. Perhaps it is this good energy that will give the strength and the inspiration to all of us to go back into the negotiations and lobbying work in the coming week with a sense of what we have truly achieved and with the conviction that nobody can take those achievements away from us. We want to make it very clear that we are aware that we have achieved something and that we're not going to give it away.

## Fin de milenio

Fin de milenio,
cerrando el tiempo recuento,
a la par de los inventos:
discriminación y guerras;
y dominancias patriarcales
de intereses contrapuestos
al planeta.

Fin de milenio,
estratégicas pobrezas
e ignorancias propiciantes
del sistema,
sentaron las fortalezas
de los que se han hecho dueños
de esta era.

Naturaleza se transformó
en reservas ahogadas de ciudad,
fue un milenio de contaminación,
arrogancias y falta de visión
y de amor.

Más que nunca ahora, nos llegó la hora
de tomar conciencia y de cambiar.
más que nunca, más que nunca ahora, nos llegó la hora,
de tomar conciencia, y de decir:
Fin de milenio será
una oportunidad, para dejar atrás,
la destrucción ambiental
y la mala dirección
de los que nunca debieron gobernar.

Fin de milenio será,
Una oportunidad, para reivindicar,
Caminos de libertad,
Derechos e igualdad
Y nuestras voces, mujeres levantar!

*Letra y música: Ana Castro Calzada*

## End of millennium

End of millennium,
the closing of time
lots of inventions
lots of discrimination and wars
along with the patriarchal domination
of interests that work against
the planet.

End of millennium,
strategic poverties
and ignorance that favors
the system,
forming the strongholds
of those who have made themselves owners
of the era.

Nature is transformed
into reserves that are smothered by the city.
It was a millennium of pollution,
arrogance, lack of vision,
lack of love.
Now, more than ever, the time has come
To become conscious and change.
Now, more than ever, the time has come
To become conscious and say:

The end of the millennium will be
an opportunity to leave
environmental destruction,
and the bad leadership
of those who never
should have governed
behind.

The end of the millennium will be
an opportunity to reclaim
the roads to freedom,
rights and equality,
along with
our voices.

Women, Rise up!

*Ana Castro Calzada is a member of Claroscuro, a feminist, all-woman musical group based in Costa Rica.*

*Words and music by Ana Castro Calzada. Reprinted by permission of author.*

# Beijing + 5 Analysis

# Taking Stock: Women's Human Rights Five Years After Beijing

*Charlotte Bunch*

ONE OF THE MOST REMARKABLE ACHIEVEMENTS OF THE PAST thirty years has been the widespread growth of women's movements around the world and the ways in which feminist questions have altered roles, relationships and public debates in almost every corner of the globe. While this clearly remains an unfinished revolution, it is these changes and the backlash against them that provide the framework for assessing the significance and outcome of the Beijing + 5 Review. We must place this at times frustrating review process in the larger context of women's organizing, particularly around the United Nations world conferences over the past quarter-of-a-century.

Since the 1960s, and with added impetus from the 1975 International Women's Year World Conference in Mexico City, women have been raising consciousness about their status in every region of the world. Women have put dozens of new issues on the world's agenda, and have sought to alter the way in which many global questions are viewed. Women are on the agenda worldwide in every field of study and in every area of public life. Abuses and neglect that once were ignored as routine are now being challenged, and that is major progress. The proof of change is the list of fights we are waging: against domestic violence, marital rape, incest, genital mutilation, sexual harassment, enforced heterosexuality, forced pregnancy, femicide, trafficking in humans and every kind of humiliation we once were told was "just life; just a woman's lot." We are fighting for women's rights to education, to reproductive and other health care choices, to property, land, and inheritance, to political participation, equal pay, and an equal voice in decision-making on all issues. All of these inalienable rights were once denied us without a second thought. Not only are we now on the agenda, we are working to transform that agenda. The fact that there is opposition to a movement for such basic changes should not, therefore, come as a surprise.

In the decade between the 1985 Third World Conference on Women in Nairobi and the 1995 Fourth World Conference in Beijing, women's networks formed regionally and globally that succeeded in advancing women's voices and perspectives on global issues in many arenas. Among the most visible of these efforts has been women's organizing to put gender on the agenda at UN world conferences in the 1990s, from the Earth Summit in Rio (1992) to the Human Rights Conference in Vienna (1993), the Cairo International Conference on Population and Development (1994), the Copenhagen Summit for Social Development (1995), the Habitat Conference in Istanbul (1996), and the World Food Summit in Rome (1997). These efforts have established women as a global force and demonstrated our potential in others.

The Beijing Women's Conference was a high point in this process with more people attending both the inter-governmental proceedings and the parallel NGO Forum than any other UN world conference to date—in spite of efforts by some to boycott and by the Chinese government to discourage participation. In Beijing, 189 governments made a broad range of promises to uphold the human rights of the three billion people who are female. The Beijing Platform for Action was a veritable referendum on the human rights of women in twelve critical areas of concern, ranging from socioeconomic rights, like poverty and education, to political participation and violence against women at home and in armed conflict. Beijing firmly established that women's rights are human rights and that meeting women's needs is central to every nation's progress in economic development and democracy.

As women have become more forceful in the global arena, inevitably, there has been resistance. The backlash against women did not start in the 1990s, but it has grown with the emergence of an unholy alliance of forces that work to defeat women's growing self-determination and political power, nationally and internationally. Whether they operate under the guise of Christian, Muslim or other religious fundamentalisms, or as right wing U.S. Republicans or nationalistic forces in ethnic conflicts around the world, they are united to oppose women's growing strength and advances towards self-determination at the global level. The battles waged were particularly intense in Cairo and

Beijing around the issues of reproductive and sexual rights; and these forces came back with a vengeance in the "plus five" reviews of these two pivotal conferences in 1999 and 2000.

## What Happened in the Beijing + 5 Process

The United Nations meeting to measure progress five years after the Fourth World Conference on Women became yet another site in the global contest over women's roles and rights. But the tension surrounding the Beijing + 5 process did not only come from the classic "feminist versus fundamentalist" showdown. Since Beijing, the impact of globalization has also exacerbated conflicts between rich and poor nations and increased many states' insecurity about their ability to control their own destinies. Furthermore, advances in international human rights law and increased efforts to hold individuals accountable for war crimes—highlighted by such events as the creation of an International Criminal Court and the indictment of General Pinochet of Chile— have brought to the surface the tension between the UN's commitment to uphold human rights while, at the same time, respecting national sovereignty. Under the guise of preserving national sovereignty or cultural diversity, some governments had become leery of human rights discourse in general, as well as with regard to women.

As a result of these various factors, the political climate of the UN General Assembly in the fall of 1999 has been described by many as one of the most tense in recent memory. Since the Beijing + 5 Review was a special session of the General Assembly, it fell victim to these tensions as well. The cooperation across geopolitical lines that is necessary for reaching consensus was harder to muster this time than it had been in 1995, and the amount of political capital that most governments were prepared to expend on a review was less than what they had put into the Beijing Conference. Further, most governments were aware of how little progress they had made toward fulfilling the Beijing promises and were reluctant to make more commitments. Even assessing women's status has grown more complex with significant improvements in some areas for some women offset by economic decline and growing violence in others.

Advocates for women's rights entered the Beijing + 5 process seeking a variety of advances for women. Where the Beijing Platform was strong in some areas, like health and violence against women, the primary goal was to get governments to make more concrete commitments to fulfilling their promises by assigning benchmarks, time-bound targets, and dedicated resources. In other areas where the Platform was weaker or had neglected critical issues, women sought language addressing matters like the impact of globalization on women, HIV/AIDS, racism, discrimination based on sexual orientation, and women and peacekeeping, to name but a few. In general, the goal was to use the review process to strengthen governmental commitment and international cooperation aimed at implementing the Platform and the human rights principles embodied in it through spelling out concrete actions that should be taken at all levels—local, national, regional, and international. (For statements about some of these goals as articulated by the Center for Women's Global Leadership during the Beijing + 5 process, please see the documents in the Appendix of this book.)

However, we often found ourselves reduced to defending the turf gained in Beijing or seemingly only making incremental advances. Conservative non-governmental forces, primarily from the religious right wing in North America, were present in large numbers and worked with representatives from a handful of determined and very vocal countries and the Holy See to water down the Beijing commitments, or at least stall any efforts to go forward from them. The uneasy and complex geopolitical climate in the UN seemed to make it difficult to move the process forward. The period from the final preparatory committee meeting in March through most of the Special Session in June 2000 was characterized by long, drawn-out and tedious negotiations and stalemate. (The frustration this produced and the fear that the Beijing Platform was threatened is reflected in the speeches at the Symposium held just before the Special Session began and recorded in the first part of this book.) Finally, the many drafts and re-drafts during the negotiations and confusion about what kind of document was needed ultimately resulted in a document that was unwieldy and often hard to follow.

Given the investment that so many women around the world had made in the Beijing Platform, it was critical to defend those advances and not lose ground in this highly visible global arena. In the end, the document produced by the Beijing + 5 process does that and is probably better than the frustrating process led us to believe it would be. Most importantly, the Beijing + 5 Political Declaration reaffirms that governments have the responsibility to implement the Beijing Platform for Action, and thus the Platform remains the reference point for governmental commitment to and action on women's rights in all twelve critical areas of concern for the next decade.

While the conservative forces did not succeed in changing the Beijing Platform, they did weaken proposals for actions that governments should undertake at this time to implement it, adding qualifying phrases like "where appropriate," or saying parties should "consider" certain actions rather than calling on them to act. Many specific dates and numerical targets proposed by some governments were removed from the draft, making it harder to measure progress and hold governments accountable to their commitments. Unfortunately, a number of governments who were reluctant to be politically bound to such goals hid behind the more vocal opponents in allowing these factors to be compromised. As the NGO statement released by the Linkage Caucus on the final day of the session stated: "We regret that there was not enough political will on the part of some governments and the UN system to agree on a stronger document with more concrete benchmarks, numerical goals, time-bound targets, indicators, and resources aimed at implementing the Beijing Platform."

As the following five papers spell out in considerable detail for the areas where the Global Center concentrated its work, the document could have been better. But it could also have been a great deal worse. It does include strong stands against trafficking in women and girls, against domestic violence—including marital rape—and against so-called "honor killings." It demands that more attention be devoted to combating racism, to the ways that globalization adversely affects women, and to the devastating HIV/AIDS epidemic. It makes maternal mortality a health sector priority and affirms women's hard won goals in the Cairo + 5 review.

Finally, we cannot talk about what happened at Beijing + 5 without noting the ways in which non-governmental organizations (NGOs) utilized the occasion to engage once more with governments about their responsibilities for upholding the human rights of women. Women, and some men, participated in record numbers during the review, as they did at the World Conference on Women in Beijing—proving once more that this is an issue central to people's lives and passions. At all four regional meetings, NGOs gathered before and/or during the governmental meetings to lobby delegates and to produce statements on a wide array of concerns. At the Special Session in New York, regional caucuses and international affinity groups formed around specific issues, prepared draft language and lobbied delegates. Many women from NGOs served on governmental delegations and/or provided technical expertise on gender issues to delegations. Based on the growing NGO experience of the past decade, both working at UN conferences and in other international arenas, many of these networks have become effective at forging common positions across various geopolitical lines.

One of the most heartening aspects of this process was the significant presence of young women who organized their own caucuses as well as participating in others. Another important development was the way the NGO caucus utilized the occasion, not only to address the Beijing + 5 Review, but also to garner attention for their concerns from media and governments as well as the UN. For example, the Caucus on Women and Armed Conflict engaged UN personnel and governments in conversations about women and peacekeeping, which helped lay the groundwork for the first historic meeting on this topic, which was held by the Security Council in October 2000.

At the national level, most governments felt obliged to meet with NGOs and make reports on what they are doing to implement the Beijing Platform; many women engaged them in debates about what needs to be done in their countries to advance women's rights. Over 100 alternative reports prepared by NGOs challenged governments' rosy national reports to the UN by telling the unvarnished truth about what governments have and have not done. In addition to focusing on the debates over the inter-governmental document, women held symposia, workshops and conferences to share experiences and learn from one another about what has worked and what has not in their own countries. As in Beijing, women used the space provided by the review to network and share strategies across cultural, racial, sexual, national and other boundaries and to outline some of the challenges ahead in the unfinished agenda of achieving rights and equality for women.

## What Beijing + 5 Revealed: Towards the Future

While the processes of the Nairobi and Beijing women's conferences were also frustrating at times, they were still high points for the international women's movement in terms of defining and elaborating women's needs and rights and setting standards for what governments should do to advance women's position in the world. The Beijing + 5 Review was more sobering, as it sought to assess how much had been done towards these lofty goals in a relatively short period of time. It should come as no surprise that the process of implementing these standards and enforcing respect for rights that have been violated around the world for centuries is more difficult.

The challenges of Beijing + 5 were the same as those faced today by women's movements locally and internationally: institutional resistance and backlash, lack of political will, insufficient resources for the task at hand, cultural undertow, and the need for alternative social models and concepts that spell out women's visions for a world without discrimination and violence. It was to address such issues that we chose to hold the Women 2000 Symposium during the Beijing + 5 process. For, while fighting for words in the inter-governmental document that will maintain government commitment to women's rights as human rights, we also need to look at women's concrete strategies and actions in the world, as they seek to fulfill the promise contained in that language. It is this interface between words and actions that our approach to the Beijing + 5 Review and to this book seeks to embody.

The Beijing + 5 process raised important questions for reflection about working for women's human rights through the United Nations system. It pointed to some of the limitations of this work when governments are not really committed to the words they pen. At the same time, it reminded us of the importance of women continuing to use the public space that the UN provides. Many people are looking for better ways for the UN to conduct such reviews since this one, like most of the other "plus five" reviews of this past decade, has proven frustrating. Perhaps processes of such profound transformation as the one signaled by the UN women's conferences need a longer time frame before a realistic assessment of progress can take place.

Another issue left unanswered by this review is whether there will be another world conference on women in the future. This question is now in the hands of the Commission on the Status of Women and the Committee on Economic, Social and Cultural Rights (ECOSOC), who must determine whether to hold such an event in 2005 or at any other point in the coming decade. While the UN is talking about cutting back on world conferences, the women's conferences have proven to be a vital impetus for the growth of the women's movement and have provided opportunities—which are still all too rare—for women to meet across national and regional lines. Whether in 2005 or later, it seems critical that women maintain the push to hold another such conference within the next decade, both as a global gathering point for women's advocates and as a target that reminds governments of their accountability to their promises to the world's women.

One of the insights that this process has revealed is the importance of human rights mechanisms for women. Indeed, the human rights underpinnings of the Beijing Platform for Action came under attack, in part because women have begun to use human rights more effectively over the past decade. Some governments objected to using human rights instruments to guarantee the Platform's promises to women; but if they can deny human rights to women on cultural or national grounds, then the very concept of human rights being universal is completely undermined. We came away from Beijing + 5 with a document that did not back down on the fundamental truth that women's rights are human rights. However, the attack on this gain reminded us that realizing it is ongoing work for which we must remain vigilant. It also pointed to the importance of women utilizing the Convention on the Elimination of All Forms of Discrimination against Women (CEDAW) and all other human rights treaties, which, unlike the Beijing Platform, are legally binding obligations on the countries that sign them.

Overall, the global women's movement prevailed in the Beijing + 5 process, in spite of frustrations and obstacles. The Beijing Platform for Action was reaffirmed and governments once more pledged that it is their responsibility to work for its implementation. While there were not as many specific targets set and resources allocated as many of us sought, there were many concrete advances that women can build on as we work to implement the Platform and to hold governments accountable to their commitments to women.

The Beijing + 5 Review had its ups and downs, but it provided one more opportunity for public discussion of many issues that affect and concern women. Because of this event, the media has aired issues and perspectives locally and globally. It is women who have placed women's empowerment and human rights on the world's agenda, utilizing events like the UN world conferences as well as many other strategies. And it is women who will continue to advance this agenda. Keeping this in mind, we can say that the Beijing + 5 process provided another public moment where women demonstrated determination and strength in working to realize justice and all human rights for all women.

# CEDAW and Beijing + 5: Consolidating Women's Human Rights or Backtracking on Commitments?

*Cynthia Meillón*

## Background[1]

THE CONVENTION ON THE ELIMINATION OF ALL FORMS OF Discrimination against Women (usually referred to as the Women's Convention or CEDAW) was adopted by the United Nations in 1979. Drafted many years prior to the 1993 World Conference on Human Rights at Vienna, at which women's human rights were officially recognized, CEDAW represents an earlier and very important step in the process of understanding and approaching women's rights as human rights. At its core, the Convention seeks to promote equality between women and men and to prevent discrimination against women.

The Beijing Platform contains many parallels with CEDAW and is the first UN world conference document in which CEDAW is clearly reflected. While some areas of great importance to women's human rights were not directly addressed in CEDAW, subsequent interpretation of the document has and can continue to serve to make it a long-lasting and evolving instrument that remains relevant to women's human rights. The Committee on the Elimination of Discrimination Against Women (also called "the CEDAW Committee") has the responsibility of monitoring States parties'[2] compliance with the Women's Convention. The Committee receives submissions and makes recommendations to States parties to improve their compliance with their treaty obligations.

*Cynthia Meillón was Beijing + 5 consultant for the Center for Women's Global Leadership.*

In 1999, after nearly a decade of work by women's human rights activists, an Optional Protocol to CEDAW was approved by the UN. This additional document makes CEDAW more effective, as it contains provisions that permit women whose rights have been violated to apply directly to the CEDAW committee if they cannot receive relief and remedy in their own country.

The relationship between the Beijing Platform and CEDAW is an important one because many of the objectives of the Platform for Action are elaborations on what is contained in CEDAW. The Beijing Platform also has the effect of moving beyond CEDAW in a number of important areas. For example, violence against women is not mentioned in the CEDAW convention, as the problem had not yet received international attention at the time it was drafted. However, it is dealt with in General Recommendations that have been made over the years by the CEDAW Committee, and by making violence against women one of the twelve Critical Areas of Concern, the Beijing Platform provides further impetus for governments to make concrete commitments in this area. When taken together with the human rights conventions—the Universal Declaration of Human Rights, the International Covenant on Economic, Social and Cultural Rights, the International Covenant on Civil and Political Rights and CEDAW, as well as the documents of the other major UN conferences of the 1990s—the Beijing Platform provides a substantial vision of human rights strategies for the next decade.

## References to CEDAW in the Outcomes Document

With regard to the relationship of CEDAW to the Beijing + 5 Outcomes Document, three points can be highlighted. First, the document contains a number of provisions that specifically address CEDAW. Second, an important paragraph promoting one of the core tenets of CEDAW was dropped from the document late in the negotiations. Finally, there are a number of articles in the document that essentially call for the implementation of the principal objectives of CEDAW without actually mentioning the Convention. It is necessary, therefore, to revisit earlier versions of the Outcomes Document and the Platform itself if we are to reach an understanding of what has taken place in this area. It is also important to note that resistance to explicitly linking CEDAW with the Outcomes Document may be understood as an attempt by some States parties to weaken the document by avoiding associating it with CEDAW, which is legally binding.

Direct and indirect references to CEDAW are contained in the cluster of paragraphs numbered 68 and 69. Particularly significant are the following:

**Paragraph 68c.** "Ratify the Convention on the Elimination of All Forms of Discrimination against Women, limit the extent of any reservations to it, and withdraw reservations which are contrary to the object and purpose of the Convention or otherwise incompatible with international treaty law;"

**Paragraph 68d.** "Consider signing and ratifying the Optional Protocol to the Convention on the Elimination of All Forms of Discrimination against Women."

**A proposed Paragraph 102e. in an earlier draft was deleted late in the negotiations.** The wording of that paragraph did not contain qualifiers (such as the word "consider") which have the effect of weakening language and making compliance optional, but stated directly: "Review, by States parties, as appropriate, all existing legislation and policy to ensure their compatibility and compliance with the provisions of CEDAW and other relevant international human rights instruments as well as ensure that future legislation is also designed accordingly;"

In the Beijing Platform for Action, actions aimed at the full implementation of CEDAW are expressed in Strategic Objective 1 under Critical Area of Concern I "Human Rights of Women." The language contained in deleted Paragraph 102e. closely mirrors that of the Platform:

**Beijing Platform, Paragraph 230g.** "If they are States parties, implement the Convention by reviewing all national laws, policies, practices and procedures to ensure that they meet the obligations set out in the Convention; all States should undertake a review of all national laws, policies, practices and procedures to ensure that they meet international human rights obligations in this matter;"

CEDAW is also very specific in its requirement that national legislation be brought in line with its principles of non-discrimination:

**The preamble of Article 3 of CEDAW reads:** "States parties shall take in all fields, in particular in the political, social, economic and cultural fields, all appropriate measures, **including legislation,** to ensure the full development and advancement of women, for the purpose of guaranteeing them the exercise and enjoyment of human rights and fundamental freedoms on a basis of equality with men."

**Analysis:** The paragraph that was designed to reinforce the implementation of CEDAW was removed from the document while the paragraph that precedes it, calling for ratification of the Convention was allowed to remain. In the paragraph that followed in the negotiated document, 68d., the word "consider" is used with regard to states' acceptance of the Optional Protocol, which has the effect of making such ratification optional.

**Paragraphs 68c. and 68d.** contain the only explicit mention of CEDAW in section IV of the Outcomes Document, which sets out the actions and initiatives that are to be taken "to achieve the full and accelerated implementation of the Beijing Platform for Action."[3] However, closer examination of the document reveals that a series of paragraphs that immediately follow 68c. and 68d. provide for fulfillment of a number of CEDAW objectives without actually referring to the Convention. For example:

**Paragraph 68f.** "Develop, review and implement laws and procedures to prohibit and eliminate all forms of discrimination against women and girls;"

This paragraph appears to call for the same actions for the same reasons as deleted Paragraph 102e., but there is an important difference. Unlike Paragraph 102e., **Paragraph 68f. makes no reference to CEDAW or to the other relevant human rights instruments**, which has the effect of delinking the Outcomes Document from human rights conventions and instruments, and most particularly from CEDAW which, as noted earlier, is a legally binding document.

Further review of the document reveals several more examples that follow this pattern:

**Paragraph 68g.** "Take measures, including programmes and policies, to ensure that maternity, motherhood and parenting and the role of women in procreation are not used as a basis for discrimination nor restrict the full participation of women in society."

Measures to prevent the discrimination of women on the grounds of matrimony and maternity are covered in Article 11 of CEDAW. However, the same article also calls for the introduction of paid maternity leave and social services for parents, which some governments may wish to avoid addressing.

**Paragraph 68h.** "Ensure that national legislative and administrative reform processes, including those linked to land reform, decentralization and reorientation of the economy, promote women's rights, particularly those of rural women and women living in poverty, and take measures to promote and implement those rights through women's equal access to and control over economic resources, including land, property rights, right to inheritance, credit and traditional saving schemes, such as women's banks and cooperatives;"

**CEDAW Article 14** addresses some of the problems of rural women and specifically mentions the right of women to organize themselves into co-operatives in order to obtain access to economic opportunities, and it refers to women's right to access loans and credit.

**Article 14e.** "To organize self-help groups and co-operatives in order to obtain equal access to economic opportunities through employment or self employment;"

**Article 14g.** "To have access to agricultural credit and loans, marketing facilities, appropriate technology and equal treatment in land and agrarian reform as well as in land resettlement schemes;"

CEDAW Article 13 states that women should not be discriminated against in economic activities.

**Article 13.** "States Parties shall take all appropriate measures to eliminate discrimination against women in other areas of economic and social life in order to ensure, on a basis of equality of men and women, the same rights..."

In some ways, Outcomes Document Paragraph 68h. surpasses CEDAW. For example, CEDAW is silent on the right to inherit property and does not mention land reform, while Paragraph 68h. mentions both. Paragraph 68h. also says that national legislation should ensure access to these rights.

**Paragraph 68j.** "Take all appropriate measures to eliminate discrimination and violence against women and girls by any person, organization or enterprise;"

**CEDAW Article 1e.** "To take all appropriate measures to eliminate discrimination against women by any person, organization or enterprise;"

Except for the addition of the word "violence," Paragraph 68j. is identical to CEDAW Article 1e.

**Paragraph 68k.** "Take necessary measures for the private sector and for educational establishments to facilitate and strengthen compliance with non-discriminatory legislation."

This article has no exact parallel in CEDAW. It is interesting to note, however, that it assumes the presence of non-discriminatory legislation while the elimination of Paragraph 102e. precludes the possibility of insisting that states review their legislation for compliance with CEDAW, which prohibits discriminatory legislation.

**Paragraphs 69a.** through **69c.** are also related to CEDAW objectives as each one recommends using legislation to redress and improve the situation of women. Since these paragraphs focus on violence against women, they move CEDAW objectives forward by being explicit in linking discrimination to violence as is called for in CEDAW General Recommendation 19.[4]

**Paragraph 69a.** calls for governments to "review and revise, where appropriate, legislation with a view to introducing effective legislation including on violence against women . . ."

**Paragraph 69c.** "Treat all forms of violence against women and girls of all ages as a criminal offence punishable by law including violence based on all forms of discrimination."

**Paragraph 69d.** carries this idea over to include domestic violence: "Establish legislation and/or strengthen appropriate mechanisms to handle criminal matters relating to all forms of domestic violence, including marital rape and sexual abuse of women and girls, and ensure that such cases are brought to justice swiftly;"

**Paragraph 69e.** talks about adopting and implementing laws "and other measures as appropriate, such as policies and educational programmes, to eradicate harmful customary or traditional practices . . .which are violations of the human rights of women and girls and obstacles to the full enjoyment by women of their human rights and fundamental freedoms, and to intensify efforts, in cooperation with local women's groups, to raise collective and individual awareness on how these harmful traditional or customary practices violate women's human rights;"

**CEDAW Article 2f.** "To take all appropriate measures, including legislation, to modify or abolish existing laws, regulations, customs and practices which constitute discrimination against women."

Paragraph 69e. is, legally speaking, less strong than CEDAW Article 2f, which simply states that the States parties should take action. The concept of raising "collective and individual awareness" as set out in the last sentence is probably a reference to female genital mutilation, but could apply to other issues as well. While it gives recognition to the need to work to build consensus in long-standing areas where people are being asked to make changes, some of the areas referred to are likely to require the application of strong measures if women's lives and safety are to be ensured.

## Conclusion

Politically speaking, all of the UN human rights documents should inform what we understand about women's human rights. When CEDAW and the Beijing Platform are used together, they become a powerful tool for promoting and protecting women's human rights.

Although the Outcomes Document by no means constitutes a roll-back of advances that have been made in the area of women's human rights, it appears that an attempt has been made by some government to keep the language of CEDAW out of the document while including and promoting some of its key objectives. This is significant because, as noted above, CEDAW is a legally binding document, while the Beijing Platform is not.

The Beijing + 5 Review negotiations cannot affect the legal status of CEDAW or the decisions that will be made by its treaty monitoring committee. However, on a political level the fact that a concerted attempt was made by many governments to keep references to CEDAW and the other human rights instruments out of the document is cause for concern. It implies that while governments may be willing to employ rhetoric that appears to support women's human rights, they are less willing to undertake binding obligations in this area. This trend merits close scrutiny in future UN negotiations.

## Notes

1. This analysis owes much to previous work by International Women's Rights Action Watch, particularly the publication *The CEDAW Convention and the Beijing Platform for Action: Reinforcing the Promise of the Rights Framework* by Kristen Timothy and Marsha Freeman (February 2000), to the ongoing work of Alda Facio, and to conversations with Susana Fried and Ilana Landsberg-Lewis.

2. The term "States parties" refers to those countries that have ratified the treaty.

3. *Report of the Ad Hoc Committee of the Whole of the twenty-third special session of the General Assembly,* formerly called *Further Actions and Initiatives to Implement the Beijing Declaration and the Platform for Action,* General Assembly, Official Records Twenty-third special session of the General Assembly entitled "Women 2000: Gender Equality, Development and Peace for the Twenty-First Century," (June 10, 2000). Supplement No.3 (A/S-23/10/Rev.1).

4. CEDAW General Recommendation No.19 (11th Session 1992) states: "1. Gender-based violence is a form of discrimination that seriously inhibits women's ability to enjoy rights and freedoms on a basis of equality with men."

# Beijing + 5 and Violence Against Women

*Lisa Clarke*

## Overview

THE BEIJING PLATFORM FOR ACTION RECOGNIZES THAT VIOLENCE against women both violates and impairs the enjoyment by women of their human rights and fundamental freedoms. The Platform sets out a significant number of clear and effective actions, which if implemented, would reduce the incidence of violence against women. Some of the more intense debates at Beijing took place around the use of the terms female foeticide, systematic rape (in the context of armed conflict) and forced prostitution and trafficking.

While some of the same debates from Beijing regarding violence against women resurfaced in the Beijing + 5 Review (for example those concerning prostitution and trafficking) there were many new elements as well. At times both governments and NGOs were frustrated with the lack of expertise in the area of gender on the part of some delegates. Yet the Beijing + 5 negotiations demonstrate a considerable improvement in awareness and consensus with regard to ending violence against women. However, despite greater understanding of the need to diminish and eliminate violence against women, there has been little concrete progress made towards this end. Women's human rights advocates lobbied for a Beijing + 5 document that would contain concrete benchmarks and time-bound targets. As in Beijing, very few time bound

*Lisa Clarke is a Program Assistant at the Center for Women's Global Leadership.*

targets and measurable goals were established, although many of the paragraphs were aimed at providing further direction for hastening the implementation of the Beijing Platform. However, as was the case at Beijing, the absence of measurable goals in the form of targets and benchmarks is a factor that continues to limit the strength of the document.

Thanks to the lobbying of advocates, the final Outcomes Document highlights achievements that have been made in relation to the commitments contained in the Beijing Platform for Action. Paragraph 13 recognizes the role women's organizations and NGOs have played in raising and promoting awareness about violence against women and supporting women who are vulnerable to violence. Much of the progress that has been made towards diminishing and eliminating violence against women can be attributed to the work of women's NGOs.

Even after agreeing that one of the major obstacles to eliminating violence against women is the lack of adequate data and the subsequent lack of understanding of the root causes and consequences of violence against women (Paragraph 14), governments still resisted establishing ways of gathering comprehensive and/or accurate data on violence against women. In keeping with the general tone of the review process, governments were reluctant to agree to statements which would involve them in internationally uniform indicators to measure violence against women, since this would make them subject to international monitoring.

Although governments have been quick to publicly agree that violence against women should be eliminated, they continue to be negligent in providing resources to support programs or develop mechanisms to address all forms of violence against women. This lack of political will demonstrated by many governments remains an ongoing concern.

However, despite the difficulties, the Outcomes Document shows some significant advances with regard to understanding violence against women and contains many forward-looking commitments by governments. The following are some examples of this progress.

## Advances from the Beijing Platform for Action in the Outcomes Document:

- **Crimes in the Name of Honour** are addressed for the first time in an international consensus document (69e., 96a.).
- The document contains stronger language on **dowry-related violence and deaths** (96a.).

- There is a call for legislation and stronger mechanisms to address **marital rape** (96d.).
- **Racially-motivated violence** against women is addressed (69g.).
- **Acid attacks** are recognized as a form of violence (96a.).
- The document calls on governments to treat all forms of **violence against women as a criminal offence,** including those based on all forms of discrimination (69c.).
- Governments are asked to consider launching a **zero tolerance campaign** on violence against women (87b.).

## Analysis
## Newly Recognized Forms of Violence Against Women: Debates and Conclusions
### Crimes Committed in the Name of Honour

**Paragraph 69e.** "Develop, adopt and fully implement laws and other measures as appropriate, such as policies and educational programmes, to eradicate harmful customary or traditional practices including female genital mutilation, early and forced marriage, and **so called honour crimes** that are violations of the human rights of women and girls, obstacles to the full enjoyment by women of their human rights and fundamental freedoms and to intensify efforts, in cooperation with local women's groups, to raise collective and individual awareness on how these harmful traditional or customary practices violate women's human rights;"

**Paragraph 96a.** "Increase cooperation, policy responses, effective implementation of national legislation and other protective and preventive measures aimed at the elimination of violence against women and girls, especially all forms of commercial sexual exploitation, as well as economic exploitation, including inter alia, trafficking in women and children, female infanticide, **crimes committed in the name of honour, crimes committed in the name of passion,** racially motivated crimes, abduction and sale of children, dowry related violence and deaths, acid attacks and harmful traditional or customary practices such as FGM, early and forced marriages;"

**Commentary:** While the expansion of the list from the Beijing Platform for Action of the different forms that violence against women can take is laudable, there was much confusion during the Beijing + 5 negotiations over how to describe such crimes which should be considered "traditional and customary practices." For example, one of the advances during the Beijing + 5 Review was the recognition of crimes committed in the name of honour. Unfortunately, however, Paragraph 69e. discusses "so called honour crimes" and paragraph

96a. addresses "crimes committed in the name of honour, crimes committed in the name of passion."

The latter paragraph contains the same wording used earlier in the year at the Commission on Human Rights, in Resolution 2000/45 on Violence Against Women, which referred to "crimes committed in the name of honour, crimes committed in the name of passion." But the confusion was not limited to nomenclature; there was also uncertainty about how to categorize this form of violence against women. Many delegations spoke of these crimes as harmful customary and traditional practices. Not only is this categorization inaccurate, it is also dangerous. Crimes committed in the name of honour and passion that result in physical or emotional battering or killing of women are crimes that should be punishable by law. Categorizing such acts as customary or traditional practices undermines the severity of these crimes and implies different strategies for eliminating this type of violence against women.

## Acid Attacks

**Paragraph 96a.** "Increase cooperation, policy responses, effective implementation of national legislation and other protective and preventive measures aimed at the elimination of violence against women and girls, especially all forms of commercial sexual exploitation, as well as economic exploitation, including *inter alia*, trafficking in women and children, female infanticide, crimes committed in the name of honour, crimes committed in the name of passion, racially motivated crimes, abduction and sale of children, dowry related violence and deaths, **acid attacks** and harmful traditional or customary practices such as FGM, early and forced marriages;"

**Commentary:** There is no mention of acid attacks in the Beijing Platform for Action, but such forms of violence against women have received increased publicity in recent years. Not only does the Outcomes Document recognize acid attacks as a form of violence against women, but it calls for governments to act to punish and eliminate this behavior.

## Moving Beyond the Beijing Platform
### Violence Against Women Based on Discrimination as a Criminal Offence

**Paragraph: 69c.** "Treat all forms of violence against women and girls of all ages as a criminal offence punishable by law including violence based on all forms of discrimination."

**Commentary:** Since the Beijing Platform for Action does not overtly refer to criminalizing violence against women based on discrimination, this paragraph represents an important advance which can be employed to address violence against women that occurs because of any form of discrimination. For example, there are many countries that recognize and take into account discrimination on the basis of sexual orientation. This paragraph can be understood as calling on governments to criminalize and punish perpetrators of violence against lesbians or bisexual women.

## Marital Rape

**Paragraph 69d.** "Establish legislation and/or strengthen appropriate mechanisms to handle criminal matters relating to all forms of domestic violence, including marital rape and sexual abuse of women and girls, and ensure that such cases are brought to justice swiftly;"

**Commentary:** While the Beijing Platform for Action recognizes marital rape as a form of violence against women, it contains no actions for addressing the abuse. Paragraph 69d. of the Outcomes Document does this and calls on governments to establish or strengthen legislation that addresses this form of abuse.

## Racism

**Paragraph 69g.** "Take measures to address through policies and programmes, racism and racially motivated violence against women and girls;"

**Paragraph 96c.** "Provide support to NGOs, in collaboration with the UN system, inter alia through regional and international cooperation, including women's organizations, and community groups in addressing all forms of violence against women and girls, including for programmes to combat race and ethnic-based violence against women and girls;"

**Commentary:** While the Beijing Platform for Action (Paragraph 118.) recognizes that women can experience violence because of their race, there are no corresponding actions suggested to address racially motivated violence. The Outcomes Document, however, calls for policies and programmes to address racism and racially motivated violence against women and girls (69g.). Furthermore, it calls for increased cooperation, policy responses, effective implementation of national legislation and other protective and preventive measures to eliminate violence against women, including racially motivated crimes (96a.). The Outcomes Document also calls for governments to take steps to address violence against indigenous women. One of the losses that women's human rights advocates had felt after Beijing was that many of the references to race and ethnicity (especially in relation to data gathering) had been replaced with the more vague "demographic factors." The more explicit reference to racism in the Beijing + 5 document represents a marked improvement.

### Forced Marriages
Paragraphs 69c. and 96a., see above.

**Paragraph 70a.** "Take appropriate measures to address the root factors, including external factors, that encourage trafficking in women and girls for prostitution and other forms of commercialized sex, forced marriages and forced labour in order to eliminate trafficking in women, including by strengthening existing legislation with a view to providing better protection of the rights of women and girls and to punishing the perpetrators, through both criminal and civil measures;"

**Commentary:** The actions in the Outcomes Document, 96a., 69d., and 70a., to end forced marriage, are stronger than those in the Platform for Action.

### Points of Greatest Resistance
### *State Accountability and Due Diligence*
**Paragraph 13. Achievements:** "It is widely accepted that violence against women and girls, whether it occurs in public or private life, is a human rights issue. It is accepted that violence against women where perpetrated or condoned by the State or its agents constitutes a human rights violation. It is also accepted that States have an obligation to exercise due diligence to prevent, investigate, and punish acts of violence whether those acts are perpetrated by the state or private persons and to provide protection to victims. There is increased awareness and commitment to prevent and combat violence against women and girls, including domestic violence, which violates and impairs or nullifies the enjoyment of their human rights and fundamental freedoms through, inter alia, improved legislation, policies and programmes."

**Paragraph 68j.** "Take all appropriate measures to eliminate discrimination and violence against women and girls by any person, organization or enterprise;"

**Commentary:** Many delegations resisted language that held states accountable for gender-based violence at the national or international level. Throughout the negotiations, governments consistently sought clarification on language regarding state responsibility. They were concerned with the accuracy and consequences of categorizing all violence against women as a human rights violation. Governments argued that acts of private individuals cannot be characterized as violations but rather that only the failure of states to act constitutes a human rights violation. This created some confusion, and many women's human rights advocates were concerned that governments were backing off from considering violence against women a human rights issue. The resistance to governmental accountability or governmental ability to hold other individuals or enterprises accountable is seen in the transformation of Paragraph 68j. The paragraph had originally read, "Ensure that all actors are held accountable for promoting and protecting the human rights of women." In the final document, this paragraph reads "Take all appropriate measures to eliminate discrimination and violence against women and girls by any person, organization or enterprise." The obligation of states in Paragraph 13. is also limited and does not sufficiently cover violence by all actors. It is stated in the Beijing Platform for Action that states are also obliged to exercise due diligence in relation to violence against women committed by companies, organizations and institutions. The resistance to including state responsibility for non-state actors was not only limited to violence against women. There is little mention of including non-state actors in the context of implementation of the Platform. The current rise in the number and and in the economic power of non-state actors (such as transnational corporations) seems to require more development of how to hold non-state actors accountable.

### *Time-Bound Targets*
**Paragraph 87b.** "Consider launching an international 'zero tolerance' campaign on violence against women."

**Commentary:** Throughout the negotiations, resistance to establishing time bound targets and measurable goals was the norm. For example, Paragraph 87b. previously read "Launch an international 'zero tolerance' campaign concerning violence against women by the end of 2001." In the final text, the date was dropped and the word "consider" was added.

### *International Data Collection*
**Paragraph 69f.** "Continue to undertake research to develop a better understanding of the root causes of all forms of violence against women in order to design programmes and take measures towards eliminating these forms of violence;"

**Paragraph 70d.** "Consider setting up or strengthening a national coordinating mechanism, for example, a national rapporteur or an inter-agency body, with participation of the civil society including NGOs, to encourage the exchange of information and to report on data, root causes, factors and trends in violence against women, in particular trafficking;"

**Paragraph 77b.** "Regularly compile and publish crime statistics and map trends in law enforcement concerning violations of the rights of women and girls to increase awareness in order to develop more effective policies."

**Paragraph 92b.** "Develop with the full participation of all countries an international consensus on indicators and ways to measure violence against women, and consider establishing a readily accessible database on statistics, legislation, training models, good practices, lessons learned and other resources with regard to all forms of violence against women, including women migrant workers;"

**Commentary:** In preparation for the Beijing + 5 Review, the Center for Women's Global Leadership prepared a *Working Paper on a Human Rights Based Approach to the Beijing + 5 Review,* in which we stated that there is a need for international cooperation and national attention to gathering data on violence against women. Uniform indicators and standards by which to establish benchmarks and measure the progress made toward the goal of diminishing and eliminating violence against women simply do not exist. Inadequate data on violence further impedes informed policy making and efforts to eliminate it. Yet, while a number of paragraphs above refer to data, many governments resisted language that would call for the formulation of international uniform standards and indicators on violence against women (92b.).

### Listing Forms of Violence against Women

**Paragraph 14.** "This makes women and girls vulnerable to many forms of violence, such as physical, sexual and psychological violence occurring in the family, including battering, sexual abuse of female children in the household, dowry related violence, marital rape, female genital mutilation and other traditional practices harmful to women, non-spousal violence and violence related to exploitation."

**Paragraph 59.** "Violence against women and girls is a major obstacle to the achievement of the objectives of gender equality, development and peace. Violence against women both violates and impairs or nullifies the enjoyment by women of their human rights and fundamental freedoms. Gender-based violence, such as battering and other domestic violence, sexual abuse, sexual slavery and exploitation, and international trafficking in women and children, forced prostitution and sexual harassment, as well as violence against women, resulting from cultural prejudice, racism and racial discrimination, xenophobia, pornography, ethnic cleansing, armed conflict, foreign occupation, religious and anti-religious extremism and terrorism are incompatible with the dignity and worth of the human person and must be combated and eliminated."

**Paragraph 96a.** "Increase cooperation, policy responses, effective implementation of national legislation and other protective and preventive measures aimed at the elimination of violence against women and girls, especially all forms of commercial sexual exploitation, as well as economic exploitation, including *inter alia* trafficking in women and children, female infanticide, crimes committed in the name of honour, crimes committed in the name of passion, racially motivated crimes, abduction and sale of children, dowry related violence and deaths, acid attacks and harmful traditional or customary practices such as FGM, early and forced marriages;"

**Commentary:** Throughout the negotiations, governments were reluctant to list the different forms of violence against women. As a result, although varying lists surfaced at different times during the negotiations, there is no one comprehensive and consistent list in the document of the various forms of violence that women experience.

### Absent in Beijing + 5: Women in Detention
*Women in Detention*

The Beijing Platform for Action recognizes that women in detention (Paragraph 116.) are targets of violence but does not specifically call on governments to address violence in this context. Despite recent recognition of the sexual and physical violence that women in detention experience, there is no mention of women in detention in the Outcomes Document.

# References to Trafficking in the Beijing + 5 Document

Cynthia Meillón

## Background

THE ISSUE OF TRAFFICKING HAS BEEN CONTENTIOUS THROUGHOUT the Beijing + 5 process, due to differing positions held by organizations committed to addressing the issue.

In 1996, the UN Special Rapporteur on Violence Against Women commissioned an international study to systematically gather information on trafficking. One outcome of the study was an attempt to broaden the understanding of trafficking to incorporate the fact that people may be trafficked for purposes other than prostitution, including domestic or manufacturing work and, in some cases, "mail order" marriages. Thus, while trafficking is generally assumed to be for the purpose of prostitution, this assumption may be problematic, as it may have the effect of rendering invisible people who are transported and/or held against their will while being exploited as forced or bonded labor in other sectors.

In approaching the issue of trafficking, it should be recognized that there are two dominant positions and that both are linked to the way prostitution is viewed. One position holds that under no circumstance can prostitution ever be viewed as work and that it can never be freely chosen as a labor activity. In other words, force or coercion—albeit tacit or circumstantial—is always pres-

*Cynthia Meillón was Beijing + 5 consultant for the Center for Women's Global Leadership.*

ent wherever prostitution is found. Proponents of this position also insist that prostitution *per se* is an act of violence against women. This position, therefore, would include both "trafficking" and "prostitution" in lists of acts of violence against women.

The other position holds that prostitution can be a labor activity that some people may choose as a means of earning a livelihood or supplementing their income from other sources, particularly given the limited number of "choices" many women face in their lives. In other words, one need not assume the presence of coercion in all situations where prostitution is being practiced. This position can, therefore, accept the concept of "sex work" as it is termed in some circles. Following from this, sex workers are workers who should have access to the same rights as other workers and their full human rights should be protected in all areas of their lives.

Throughout Beijing + 5, proponents of the first position focused on sections in the document that address violence against women and girls, where they sought to have both trafficking and prostitution included in lists of acts of violence against women. The opposing view rejects the inclusion of all forms of prostitution in such lists, claiming that this would allow governments to equate "the elimination of prostitution" with efforts to eliminate all forms of violence against women, and that this process has, in practice, led to abusive activities against women and girls. Furthermore, some proponents of this position are concerned that discourse against trafficking may be being used to mask government activity that is actually anti-immigration and anti-immigrant, and that efforts to stop trafficking could, in some cases, be used as an excuse to limit women's freedom of movement and travel.

A third position at Beijing + 5 held that since this debate will not be resolved in the near future, it should take place outside of the Beijing + 5 setting so that participants might address concrete ways to prevent those areas and aspects of prostitution that are clearly "forced" and issues of trafficking within the broader context of violence against women without being stalemated over one area of disagreement.

**References to Trafficking and Related Issues**
References to trafficking and sexual slavery are included in fifteen paragraphs of the Outcomes Document. However, the issue is most substantively treated in Paragraphs 70a. through 70d. (under "Actions to be taken at the national level by Governments") and in Paragraphs 96a. through 97c. (under "Actions to be taken at the national and international levels by Governments, regional and

international organizations, including the United Nations system, and international financial institutions and other actors, as appropriate"). This document will focus mainly on these paragraphs, which contain the principal and most developed references to the issue.

References to trafficking also appear in paragraphs on violence against women in Section II "Achievements and Obstacles in the implementation of the twelve critical areas of the Platform for Action" (Paragraphs 14., 15., 16., 32. and 33.) and in Section III "Current Challenges affecting the full implementation of the Beijing Declaration and the Platform for Action" (Paragraph 41.).

**Paragraph 70a.** instructs governments to "take appropriate measures to address the root factors, including external factors, that encourage trafficking in women and girls for prostitution and other forms of commercialized sex, forced marriages and forced labour in order to eliminate trafficking in women, including by strengthening existing legislations with a view to providing better protection of the rights of women and girls and to punishing the perpetrators, through both criminal and civil measures;"

**Paragraph 41.** in the section on "Current Challenges" states: "The patterns of migratory flows of labour are changing. Women and girls are increasingly involved in internal, regional and international labour migration to pursue many occupations....While this situation increases their earning opportunities and self-reliance, it also exposes them, particularly the poor, uneducated, unskilled and/or undocumented migrants, to inadequate working conditions, increased health risk, the risk of trafficking, economic and sexual exploitation..." Paragraph 41. is theoretically linked to Paragraph 70a. Significantly, neither paragraph draws conclusions about the reasons women find it necessary to migrate in increasing numbers, thus evading any mention of the structural underpinnings of economic inequality.

**Analysis:** Paragraph 70a. was considerably altered during the last part of the negotiations. Its final form reflects language contained in the report on the findings of the international investigation on trafficking in women, forced labour and slavery-like practices in the context of marriage, domestic labour and prostitution that was carried out in 1996 for the UN Special Rapporteur on Violence Against Women. In that report, the Special Rapporteur stated: "...the reality is that modern manifestations of trafficking include persons trafficked into forced labour, bonded labour, and servitude."[1] The language in this paragraph represents a compromise from language that was suggested earlier in the negotiations, which included a more explicit listing of activities for which people might be trafficked, and which had the effect of narrowing the focus of trafficking.

**Paragraph 70b.** This paragraph contains a commitment to take effective measures, at the national level, "to eliminate all forms of trafficking in women and girls through a comprehensive anti-trafficking strategy consisting of *inter alia,* legislative measures, prevention campaigns, information exchange, **assistance and protection for and reintegration of the victims** and prosecution of all the offenders involved, including intermediaries."

The content of Paragraph 70b. is reiterated for the international level in **Paragraph 96c.** "As appropriate, pursue and support national, regional and international strategies to reduce the risk to women and girls, including those who are refugees and displaced persons, as well as women migrant workers, of becoming victims of trafficking; strengthen national legislation by further defining the crime of trafficking in all its elements and by reinforcing the punishment accordingly; enact social and economic policies and programmes, as well as informational and awareness-raising initiatives, to prevent and combat trafficking in persons, especially women and children; prosecute perpetrators of trafficking; **provide measures to support, assist and protect trafficked persons in their countries of origin and destination; and facilitate their return to and support their reintegration into their countries of origin.**"

While both paragraphs mention taking measures to end trafficking and providing assistance and protection for victims of trafficking, neither contains the type of comprehensive preventative and compensatory measures for victims of trafficking that were recommended in the "Agreed Conclusions" document of the Economic Commission for Europe (ECE) Regional Preparatory Meeting for Beijing + 5, January 2000), which states that governments should develop policies to "strengthen women's social and economic position" and promote "grants to NGOs to accelerate the empowerment of women in all areas of society." The ECE document also recommends that victims of trafficking not only be free from prosecution but that countries "consider allowing victims of trafficking [to] remain within the country of destination on humanitarian and compassionate grounds, in appropriate cases..." Governments are also supposed to take measures to protect the security of victims and their families, and to provide them with basic services, including shelter and health care.[2]

**Paragraph 70c.** "Consider preventing, within the legal framework and in accordance with national policies, victims of trafficking, particularly women and girls, from being prosecuted for their illegal entry or residence, taking into account that they are victims of exploitation;"

While this paragraph offers the possibility of not prosecuting victims of trafficking "for their illegal entry or residence" it by no means guarantees that this will not take place. This language is identical to that of the ECE document under "Strategic direction 3: Protecting and supporting victims of trafficking." The presence of the word "consider" leaves states parties considerable leeway and to do so or not also hinges on national policy. (It is worth bearing in mind that national policy may change when political administrations change and that, in the case of the European Commission, is in fact, not national, but rather, regional.) Furthermore, in the ECE document, this point is followed by one that provides that governments may "consider allowing victims of trafficking to remain within the country of destination on humanitarian and compassionate grounds, in appropriate cases," while the Outcomes Document contains no clause to this effect.

**Paragraph 96a.** under "Actions to be taken at the national and international level" states: "Increase cooperation, policy responses, effective implementation of national legislation and other protective and preventive measures aimed at the elimination of violence against women and girls, especially all forms of commercial sexual exploitation, as well as economic exploitation, including trafficking in women and children..." It is linked to **Paragraph 97a.**, which states: "Intensify cooperation between States of origin, transit and destination to prevent, suppress and punish trafficking in persons, especially women and children;" and **Paragraph 97b.**, which supports the negotiations on "a draft protocol to prevent, suppress and punish trafficking in persons, especially women and children, to supplement the draft UN Convention against Transnational Organized Crime."[3]

**Paragraph 97c.** outlines strategies for eliminating and punishing trafficking. Interestingly, it calls for "further defining the crime of trafficking in all its elements." This paragraph calls for the enactment of "social and economic policies and programmes...to prevent and combat trafficking in persons..." It also calls for "measures to support, assist and protect trafficked persons in countries of origin and destination" and says that States parties must "facilitate their return to and support their reintegration in countries of origin." This last phrase again omits any clause suggesting that trafficked persons may wish or need to remain in the country of destination. None of the paragraphs cited above contains any concrete or comprehensive measures for providing needed essential services to trafficked persons.

## Other paragraphs containing references to Trafficking
### Section D. Violence against Women

**Paragraph 14.**, *Obstacles.* The final sentence of this paragraph states: "It is also noted that in some countries, problems have arisen from the use of new information and communication technologies for trafficking in women and children and for the purposes of all forms of economic and sexual exploitation."

This reflects the concern felt by some anti-trafficking advocates that the internet is a key factor (rather than one of many factors) facilitating trafficking and the commercial sex industry. This is part of a larger, ongoing debate as to how, and to what extent, new communications technologies should be regulated.

### Section E. Women and Armed Conflict

**Paragraph 15.** *Achievements.* This paragraph applauds the adoption of the Rome Statute of the International Criminal Court, making specific reference to "sexual slavery" and "enforced prostitution" as war crimes and—under some undefined circumstances—crimes against humanity, when committed in the context of armed conflict.

This is a positive inclusion in that it reinforces the paragraphs on gender-based violence contained in the ICC document at a moment when opposing forces are seeking to undermine this important aspect of the Statute. **Paragraph 19.**, includes "sexual slavery" in a list of forms of sexual violence women experience: "There has been an increase in all forms of violence against women, including sexual slavery, rape, systematic rape, sexual abuse and forced pregnancies, in situations of armed conflict." The last sentence of the paragraph states: "Girls are also abducted or recruited, in violation of international law, into situations of armed conflict including as combatants, sexual slaves or providers of domestic services," which serves to reinforce the language in Paragraph 12.

### Conclusion

In general, language on trafficking contained in the document reflects a balanced position, though perhaps one not as vigorous as some advocates would like to see. It should be admitted that trafficking is a growing phenomenon for which no conclusive deterrent has been found. Among women's human rights activists there are some who have a well-grounded fear that measures to halt trafficking could have a discriminatory effect on women who are "poor, uneducated, unskilled and/or undocumented," as enunciated in Paragraph 32. of the Outcomes Document, at the same time that measures need to be taken to protect people from trafficking. It seems unlikely that any solution that does not address the real "root causes" of trafficking (i.e. economic and political situations that render people vulnerable to abuse during their pursuit of survival) can be truly effective. In the meantime, people will continue to put themselves at risk as long as their economic rights are not guaranteed. To this effect, it is important that women's human rights activists were present at the debates on the protocol to the Convention against Transnational Organized Crime, seeking to prevent efforts to halt trafficking from having inadvertent negative consequences for already vulnerable women and girls.[4]

## Notes

1. A/AC.254/CRP.13, pp.16-17.

2. *Draft Report,* Economic Commission for Europe, Regional Preparatory Meeting on the 2000 Review of Implementation of the Beijing Platform for Action, 19–21 January 2000. E/ECE/RW.2/2000/CRP.1 (January 20, 2000).

3. See UN General Assembly resolution 54/126.

4. Negotiations for the Protocol to Prevent, Suppress and Punish Trafficking in Persons were completed in October 2000.

# Beijing +5: Respecting, Promoting and Protecting Women's Diversities

Lisa Clarke and Cynthia Rothschild

## I. Sexual Orientation and Sexual Rights
### The Public Debate on Sexual Orientation during Beijing + 5

SEXUAL ORIENTATION WAS NOT INCLUDED ANYWHERE IN THE BEIJING Platform for Action. During the negotiations some delegations were opposed to including language around sexual orientation, as they said that it would create a "new right." The proposed language, however, never referred to sexual orientation as a right. Rather, it cited sexual orientation as a basis of discrimination, which prevents some women from fully enjoying their rights. While, in the end, explicit references to sexual orientation were deleted, sixteen countries from all regions stated that they would interpret the relevant clauses of the Beijing Platform for Action, in particular Paragraph 96. (quoted below in Paragraph 72k. of the Beijing + 5 Outcomes Document) to include protections around sexual orientation.

In the end, no consensus was reached on references to sexual orientation during the June 2000 UN Special Session on Beijing + 5. Language similar to that proposed in Paragraph 102j. (calling for the review and repeal of laws criminalizing homosexuality, because such laws encourage violence against women) was adopted by the final report of the Economic Commission for Europe (ECE)

*Lisa Clarke is a Program Assistant at the Center for Women's Global Leadership. Cynthia Rothschild is a writer and activist who helped to coordinate the Lesbian Caucus and sexuality programming at Beijing + 5.*

Regional Preparatory Meeting for Beijing + 5, in January 2000. At that time, no ECE country, neither governments nor the Holy See, made any reservation to this consensus. Further, the Lima Consensus from the Economic Commission for Latin American and Caribbean (ECLAC) Regional Preparatory Meeting (February 2000) calls for countries to undertake to "guarantee the protection of women's human rights, including the sexual and reproductive rights and address violations of these rights, with particular attention to all forms of gender-based violence and its root causes, including the reproduction of a culture of violence."

## *Grueling Negotiations*

In building on the support shown during the ECE and ECLAC meetings, women's human rights groups called for protection against violence, protection against discrimination, and respect for diversity. However, in order to avert references to sexual orientation, some of the more conservative delegations wanted to remove any listing of additional barriers that women face to the enjoyment of their human rights out of concern that the phrase "full diversity of women" was a smokescreen for sexual orientation. After much debate over the placement of such a list, a listing of the barriers women face was placed in the introduction to the final document (Paragraph 5.). Throughout the negotiations, sexual orientation had appeared in brackets in this list and was only finally excluded from the list on the last night of the negotiations. The list does include the words "other status," which many governments have said they would interpret to include sexual orientation.

As in Beijing, the debate over sexual rights was heated and contentious. One of the arguments used was that while the financially secure North could support sexual rights advocacy, the developing South had more pressing issues which needed attention. Opponents of sexual rights strategically deployed sexuality to foster this division by attempting to portray sexuality as a new, superficial human rights issue which is not of interest to the South, and as a "roadblock" in the negotiation process. However, delegates and NGO representatives from all regions continued to support sexual rights advocacy as a fundamental component of their human rights work. Many such groups recognized the importance of local sexual rights advocacy and made conceptual links between discrimination, violence against women, and the need for sexual rights advocacy; and many recognized the regional and cultural breadth of sexual rights work. Although the final text negotiations did not result in secure gains for sexual rights advocacy, these supportive positions were voiced throughout the Beijing + 5 process from a number of governments.

## Analysis
### Sexual Orientation, Discrimination and Violence

**Paragraph 68f.** "Develop, review and implement laws, procedures to prohibit and eliminate all forms of discrimination against women and girls;"

**Paragraph 69c.** "Treat all forms of violence against women and girls of all ages as a criminal offence punishable by law including violence based on all forms of discrimination;"

**Commentary:** While there are no overt references to sexual orientation in the Outcomes Document, many governments stated that they would interpret "other status" to include sexual orientation. In doing so, Canada referred to the United Nations Human Rights Committee 1994 decision, *Nicholas Toonen v. Australia,* which holds that protections against discrimination in the International Convention on Civil and Political Rights must be understood to include sexual orientation. In addition, a number of countries have passed legislation prohibiting discrimination on the basis of sexual orientation. In recent years, two countries, Ecuador and South Africa, have included such protections in their constitutions. Protections against discrimination based on sexuality and sexual orientation have been widely affirmed by UN bodies, including the Office of the High Commissioner for Human Rights, the UN High Commissioner for Refugees, the UN Human Rights Committee, the UN Special Rapporteur on Violence Against Women and the UN Special Rapporteur on Extrajudicial, Summary or Arbitrary Executions.

### Sexual Rights

**Paragraph 72k.** (Paragraph 96. of the Platform for Action) "The human rights of women include their right to have control over and decide freely and responsibly on matters related to their sexuality, including sexual and reproductive health, free of coercion, discrimination and violence. Equal relationships between women and men in matters of sexual relations and reproduction, including full respect for the integrity of the person, require mutual respect, consent and shared responsibility for sexual behavior and its consequences."

**Commentary:** Women's human rights advocates worked hard for the inclusion of the expression "sexual rights" in the document. This phrase was used in the Lima Consensus document, which was drawn up at the ECLAC Regional Preparatory meeting in February 2000. The phrase was not included in the final Beijing + 5 text but was supplanted with Paragraph 96. of the Beijing Platform for Action. Sexual orientation is a part of experiencing sexuality and sexual health, the purpose of which, as expressed in Paragraph 94. of the Beijing Platform for Action "is the enhancement of life and personal relations."

During a well attended panel organized by the Lesbian Caucus, representatives from conservative religious organizations passed out anti-gay and anti-reproductive rights flyers claiming "The West is Obsessed with Sex." In another flyer entitled "The West is Holding Up the Document," the slow negotiating process of Beijing + 5 was tied to sexual rights and reproductive rights advocacy: "If the West would stop pushing homosexual and abortion 'rights' on unwilling countries, the document would be done. Don't blame the developing countries with the courage to defend their values and their right to self-government!" The flyer was not attributed to any organization(s) or countries. The right-wing NGOs involved in the distribution of these fliers also claimed that the advancement of sexual rights would promote pedophilia and necrophilia.

## Sexual Orientation as Grounds for Asylum

**Paragraph 68i.** "Mainstream a gender perspective into national immigration and asylum policies, regulations and practices, as appropriate, in order to promote and protect the rights of all women, including the consideration of steps to recognize gender-related persecution and violence when assessing grounds for granting refugee status and asylum."

**Commentary:** The Outcomes Document implicitly recognizes sexual orientation as grounds for asylum because the United Nations High Commissioner for Refugees recognizes sexual orientation as a form of gender-based persecution. Under the 1951 UN Refugee Convention, asylum seekers can be granted refugee status if they are able to demonstrate a "well founded fear of persecution" in their country for "...membership of a particular social group..." A person's sexual orientation is a fundamental part of her identity. Therefore, lesbians, bisexuals and transgendered people are manifestly a "particular social group."

## Reference to the Report of the Beijing Conference

**Paragraph 1.** "The Governments which came together at the Special Session of the General Assembly have reaffirmed their commitment to the goals and objectives contained in the Beijing Declaration and the Platform for Action adopted at the IV World Conference on Women in 1995 as contained in the report of the Conference."

**Commentary:** Throughout the proceedings, some opponents of sexual orientation and sexual rights language moved to include reference to the official

Report of the Beijing Conference, rather than just the Platform for Action, since it includes the strong reservations condemning sexual and reproductive rights put forth by some states during the 1995 text negotiations. However, the Report of the Beijing Conference also contains strong statements in support of including sexual orientation and sexual rights in the document, a fact which is less known and works in the favor of sexual rights advocacy. The final Beijing + 5 document does, in fact, mention the Beijing report.

## II. The Family and Motherhood
### *The Religious Right's Obsession with "The Family"*

After extensive debates in Beijing, the Platform for Action recognizes that "various forms of the family exist" in different cultural, political and social systems and that "maternity, parenting and the role of women in procreation must not be a basis for discrimination nor restrict the full participation of women in society" (Paragraph 29.).

Tactics used by the Holy See to influence the tone of the document included peppering the text, wherever possible, with references to "strengthening the family" and "in support of the family." The Holy See and conservative religious groups claimed total ownership of the notion of "family" and "motherhood," as they have at previous conferences, including Beijing and the Cairo International Conference on Population and Development. Many references to family called for by the Holy See were deleted from the final text. Fundamentalists also wanted to see "the family" defined as a nuclear family composed of a man, a woman and their offspring. Furthermore, they championed the idea that women's most important contribution to society is that of motherhood and that a great need exists to protect the disintegrating family.

The most notable gains in this area at Beijing + 5 are as follows:

**Paragraph 20.** "There is increased awareness of the need to reconcile employment and family responsibilities and the positive effect of measures such as maternity and paternity leave and also parental leave, and child and family care services and benefits."

**Paragraph 60.** "Women play a critical role in the family. The family is the basic unit of society and is a strong force for social cohesion and integration and as such should be strengthened. The inadequate support to women and insufficient protection and support to their respective families affect society as a whole and undermines efforts to achieve gender equality. In different cultural, political and social systems, various forms of the family exist and the rights, capabilities and responsibilities of family members must be respected. Women's social and economic contributions to the welfare of the family and the social significance of maternity and paternity continue to be inadequately addressed. Motherhood and fatherhood and the role of parents and legal guardians in the family and in the upbringing of children and the importance of all family members to the family's well-being is also acknowledged and must not be a basis for discrimination. Women also continue to bear a disproportionate share of the household responsibilities and the care of children, the sick and the elderly. Such imbalance needs to be consistently addressed through appropriate policies and programmes, in particular those geared towards education and through legislation where appropriate. In order to achieve full partnership, both in public and private spheres, both women and men must be enabled to reconcile and share equally work responsibilities and family responsibilities."

**Paragraph 68g.** "Take measures, including programmes and policies, to ensure that maternity, motherhood, parenting and the role of women in procreation are not used as a basis for discrimination nor restrict the full participation of women in society;"

**Paragraph 82c.** "Develop or strengthen policies and programmes to support the multiple roles of women in contributing to the welfare of the family in its various forms, which acknowledge the social significance of maternity and motherhood, parenting, the role of parents and legal guardians in the upbringing of children and caring for other family members. Such policies and programmes should also promote shared responsibility of parents, women and men and society as a whole in this regard;"

**Paragraph 99j.** "Provide support to and empower women who play an important role within their families as stabilizing factors in conflict and post-conflict situations;"

**Commentary:** While the document makes many references to women as mothers and their role in families, the references are not as limiting as many had originally feared. Rather than asserting that women's primary role in society is motherhood, the Outcomes Document reflects the need to address the multiple roles of women in contributing to the welfare of the family in its various forms.

## III. Diversity, Culture and National Sovereignty
### Diversity at Beijing + 5
During the negotiations at Beijing, women's human rights NGOs lobbied for the recognition of discrimination based on race and ethnicity (among other factors) as barriers women face to empowerment and advancement. NGOs also called for the recognition of the multiplicity of barriers that women face.

Thanks to the lobbying of advocates, the Beijing Platform for Action mentions race and ethnicity as barriers women face to advancement (Paragraphs 48. and 226.) and acknowledges the multiple barriers women face to empowerment (Paragraph 32.). However, the listings in these paragraphs are incomplete and omit discrimination based on national origin, sexual orientation, indigenous peoples, and socioeconomic status.

**Paragraph 4.** "The Platform for Action emphasizes that women share common concerns that can be addressed only by working together and in partnership with men towards the common goal of gender equality around the world. It respects and values the full diversity of women's situations and conditions and recognizes that some women face particular barriers to their empowerment."

**Paragraph 5.** "The Platform for Action recognizes that women face barriers to full equality and advancement because of such factors as their race, age, language, ethnicity, culture, religion or disability, because they are indigenous women, or because of other status. Many women encounter specific obstacles related to their family status, particularly as single parents; and to their socio-economic status, including their living conditions in rural, isolated or impoverished areas. Additional barriers also exist for refugee women, other displaced women, including internally displaced women, as well as for immigrant women and migrant women, including women migrant workers. Many women are also particularly affected by environmental disasters, serious and infectious diseases, and various forms of violence against women."

**Commentary:** Although the Platform for Action contains a list which speaks of "The full diversity of women's situations and conditions," there was much resistance in the Beijing + 5 negotiations to the expression "the full diversity of women." Some delegations said that they would be comfortable saying "diversity" or "respect for diversity" but did not want to include a listing. At one point in the negotiations, the reference to the "full diversity of women" was deleted from the introduction. Women's NGOs lobbied arduously to have the phrase reinstated in the introduction for it is important that the entire document reflect the diverse barriers that diverse women experience to "full equality and advancement." The list appears in the final document in Paragraph 5., which is actually Paragraph 46. of the Beijing Platform for Action, verbatim.

Women's human rights advocates lobbied for an expansion of the Platform for Action's list of the barriers women face to include such factors as educational status, citizenship, marital status, sexual orientation, or because they are widows, rural women or internally displaced women. Unfortunately, the list from Beijing was not expanded. There is a reference in Paragraph 43. to the increasing number of widows, but no corresponding action suggested for hardships women endure because they are widows. Unfortunately, there was so much contention over whether a list of women's diversity should appear at all, and if so, where it should be placed, that there was never a public discussion about expanding the list. The exception, of course, was the recommendation to include sexual orientation, which was controversial.

### Diversity: A Long Standing Debate

Extensive debates took place in Beijing over the text of Paragraph 9. with regard to the balance between the universality of women's human rights and the specific role of religion and culture. Women's human rights NGOs advocated that universal human rights should not be subordinated to religion and culture. The final outcome was a compromise, which recognizes the importance of national sovereignty but locates human rights as the key concern.

**Paragraph: Previous 2bis. (now Paragraph 3.).** "The implementation of the Beijing Platform for Action as well as the further actions and initiatives contained in this document is the sovereign right of each state, consistent with national laws and development priorities, with the full respect for the various religious and ethical values and cultural backgrounds of its people, and in conformity with all human rights and fundamental freedoms."

**Agreed Paragraph 3.** "The objective of the Platform for Action, which is in full conformity with the purposes and principles of the Charter of the United Nations and international law, is the empowerment of all women. The full realization of all human rights and fundamental freedoms of all women is essential for the empowerment of women. While the significance of national and regional particularities and various historical, cultural and religious backgrounds must be borne in mind, it is the duty of States, regardless of their political, economic and cultural systems, to promote and protect all human rights and fundamental freedoms. The implementation of the Platform, as well as further actions and initiatives contained in this document, including through national laws and the formulation of strategies, policies, programmes and development priorities, is the sovereign responsibility of each State, in conformity with all human rights and fundamental freedoms, and the significance of and full respect for various religious and ethical values, cultural backgrounds and philosophical convictions of individuals and their communities should contribute to the full enjoyment by women of their human rights in order to achieve equality, development and peace."

**Commentary:** For many years, women have been calling on governments to respect, reflect, and act on the diverse needs of women. While many governments affirmed this need, there were some that called for respect for diversity only with regard to cultural diversity among states. Interestingly, the same governments that called for and supported respect for cultural diversity were the first to repudiate references to women's diversity. The previous Paragraph 2bis. (now Paragraph 3.) is not only Paragraph 5. of the Cairo + 5 review document (A/S-21/5/aa.1), which is preceded by strong language on women's human rights, but it is also identical to a paragraph rejected at Beijing. At Beijing + 5, women's human rights advocates lobbied strongly to change this paragraph. After extensive debates, the fall back decision was to quote Paragraph 9. of the Beijing Platform for Action, which asserts that implementation of the Platform for Action is the "sovereign responsibility" and duty of states.

## *Dialogue Among and Within Civilizations*

**Paragraph: Previous 48bis. (now Paragraph 95i.).** "The implementation of the Platform for Action, which aims at the empowerment and full realization of all human rights and fundamental freedoms for all women, will be enhanced by strengthening international cooperation and understanding through *inter alia* the full recognition of cultural diversity and dialogue among cultures and civilizations which the international community recognizes as essential for the achievement of the purposes of the United Nations."

**Paragraph 95i.** "Continue to design efforts for the promotion of respect for cultural diversity and dialogue among and within civilizations in a manner which contributes to the implementation of the Platform for Action, which aims at the empowerment of women and the full realization of all human rights and fundamental freedoms for all women and in a manner which ensures that gender equality and the full enjoyment of all human rights by women are not undermined;"

**Commentary:** The language calling for "respect for cultural diversity and dialogue among civilizations" was introduced by Iran. In November 1998, the General Assembly of the United Nations proclaimed the year 2001 as the "United Nations Year of Dialogue among Civilizations." The resolution GA/RES/53/22, proposed by the Islamic Republic of Iran and supported by a large number of countries, invites "Governments, the United Nations system, including the United Nations Educational, Scientific and Cultural Organization, to plan and implement appropriate cultural, educational and social programmes to promote the concept of dialogue among civilizations, including through organizing conferences and seminars and disseminating information and scholarly material on the subject." A subsequent resolution reaffirmed the provisions of the resolution GA/RES/53/22 in February 2000 (resolution 54/113). Few can argue against the statement that there is a need for greater dialogue and respect among and within nations. However, Paragraph 48bis. claims that the Platform for Action would be strengthened by "the full recognition of cultural diversity and dialogue among cultures and civilization." This formulation was vague and could permit governments to justify policies, laws and actions that are discriminatory or harmful towards women, claiming that to do so is their sovereign or cultural right. There was no clause that required that respect for varying cultural differences be compatible with the spirit and intent of the Beijing Platform for Action. Fortunately, this paragraph was favorably altered to demand that respect for cultural specificity enhance implementation of the Platform for Action (Paragraph 95i.).

# Women's Economic Rights: A Few Steps Forward and a Long Way to Go

*elmira Nazombe*

## Prologue

THE PARADOX OF THE BEIJING PLATFORM FOR ACTION IS THAT there is a distinct imbalance between its analysis of women's economic realities as multifaceted and the solutions that it proposes. The Platform for Action (PFA) builds a clear picture of the many facets of women's poverty and women's economic inequality. In the case of poverty, it identifies the negative connections of poverty and macroeconomic policy, in particular structural adjustment, debt and debt servicing as well as policies of economic transition. With regard to "women in economy," its analysis is much more sweeping. It identifies a wide range of causes, including women's absence in economic decision-making, discrimination in education and various types of labor market discrimination, and societies' failure to value unpaid work.

The PFA details several types of solutions:

1. Macroeconomic policy changes to enhance poverty eradication efforts;
2. Enhanced national employment creation strategies;
3. Expansion of opportunities for women's self-employment and entrepreneurship as well as microcredit and microenterprise;
4. Devising methods to count and value women's unpaid work.

*elmira Nazombe is Program Director at the Center for Women's Global Leadership.*

It can perhaps be said that the strongest emphasis of the PFA (35 paragraphs) and of much of the international and national efforts, have been on microcredit and microenterprise, women's self-help and entrepreneurship strategies. By comparison, there are seventeen action strategies on employment, nine of which are directed toward policy initiatives, and ten related to unpaid work and harmonization of family responsibilities.

## The Beijing + 5 Review: Globalization is Front and Center

The Beijing + 5 Review gave governments and NGOs an opportunity to revise their analysis of women's economic realities based on new developments since 1995. While globalization received some attention at Beijing in 1995, it became the defining reality for the review. The word "globalization" appears eleven times in the final Outcomes Document. Although its impacts and causes were hotly debated by governments and NGOs alike, the final document, thanks in no small measure to the persistent efforts of some NGOs towards a few key government delegations, clearly identifies globalization as a source of some positive changes, but just as clearly as a source of "deepening inequalities among and within countries," with adverse impacts on women's lives. The connections between privatization policies, declining spending for public services, the feminization of poverty and the failure to achieve gender equality are also identified.

Governments acknowledged that the gender impacts of globalization have not been systematically evaluated. There was consensus that the benefits of globalization have not been evenly distributed. They also agreed that there has been a growth of women's employment but that the negative impact of economic policies has increased job vulnerability for women. The external economic factors are seen to have contributed to the inability of states to provide social protection and social security for women. The realities of declining levels of development assistance, the high cost of debt and debt servicing, declining international terms of trade, economic restructuring and the impacts of globalization and structural adjustment programs are also named as sources of the increasing feminization of poverty and as factors undermining efforts to achieve gender equality (Paragraphs 35. and 36.).[1]

All of this represents an important step forward from the PFA and helped make possible the development of a more integrated set of action strategies at Beijing + 5.

## An Enabling Environment

Because economic policies must always exist within a broader policy framework, NGOs called on governments to create an "enabling environment" in which gender-sensitive economic policies could function. Two elements, in particular, were called for: (1) affirmation of government responsibility for upholding fundamental human rights as the basic framework for all policy; and (2) acknowledgment of the full diversity of women's realities and the differential impact of policies on them.

The Outcomes Document, while acknowledging the role of culture and national historical values, reaffirms the responsibility of governments to protect fundamental rights. Although a majority of governments were, on the whole, reluctant to repeatedly enumerate the diversity of women's experience, they agreed to a comprehensive listing in the opening paragraphs of the document. NGOs were unsuccessful in their attempts at more frequent inclusion of the phrase "women in all their diversity," which would have encouraged the implementation of action strategies that could be adapted to a diversity of women's realities (Paragraphs 3., 4. and 5.).[2]

## Gender Perspective at the Center

In the Outcomes Document, governments reaffirm the importance of a gender perspective in all phases of macroeconomic and social development policy making. NGO lobbying efforts were successful in getting the inclusion of references to the role of women and women's participation in the decision-making and implementation process as a recurring message. The phrase "guarantee equal participation of women" occurs frequently in the text. This means, at least rhetorically, putting women into the center of processes where the 1995 PFA declared they were largely absent.

## Action Strategies to Meet the Challenges of Globalization

During the review process, the Economic Justice Caucus[3] developed proposals for areas where gains would be needed in light of globalization: (1) macroeconomic policy; (2) employment and workers' rights; (3) poverty eradication; (4) economic rights; (5) entrepreneurship and microcredit; (6) harmonization of work and family responsibilities; and (7) data collection, as well as other miscellaneous concerns.

## Macroeconomic Policy

Governments of developing countries strongly supported the need for changes in the decision-making structure at the international level in order to meet the challenges of globalization. In what may have been a spillover from the Seattle WTO process, they insisted on a call for "enhanced and effective" participation in international economic decision-making. Within this broad goal there is the call for gender perspective in all policy making (especially structural adjustment and trade liberalization programs) and guarantees of equal participation of women, particularly from developing countries (Paragraphs 74c., 101a., 101b. and 101h.).[4]

The recurrent phrase is "full and effective" participation of women. However, having identified the negative effects of debt servicing and declining development assistance, the Outcomes Document merely repeats the PFA call for implementation of the 20/20 initiative[5] and 0.7 percent GDP development assistance targets.[6]

## Poverty Eradication

The Outcomes Document recognizes the need for a multiplicity of strategies on both the national and international levels. For example, skills training, equal access and control of resources, basic services, technology, and microcredit to address women's poverty and the negative social and economic effects of globalization. In addition, encouragingly, it recognizes the diversity of women living in poverty: rural women, indigenous women, female-headed households and marginalized women. Again, the "full and effective participation of women" is called for, along with the development of comprehensive gender-sensitive poverty eradication strategies to address "social, structural and macro economic issues," because of the "mutually reinforcing links between gender equality and poverty eradication."

Finally, incorporating an NGO suggestion, the document calls for the creation of social development funds to address the negative effects of Structural Adjustment Programs (SAPs), trade liberalization, and the disproportionate burden borne by women in poverty.[7]

## Employment and Workers' Rights

In an important new emphasis that reflects the document's analysis of globalization, the Outcomes Document contains a call for the extension of social protection to the new and flexible forms of work that have emerged as a result of globalization (Paragraph 74b.).[8] If seriously implemented, this strategy would help to lessen women's vulnerabilities in the many new work environments where they are being drawn. Governments also call for a multiplicity of strategies to address employment concerns, which include social protection, but also ways to address "fiscal obstacles," such as credit and microenterprise, among others (Paragraphs 75. and 82f.).[9] Also responding to globalization and other economic changes, Governments call for analysis of the differential effects of job creation and retrenchment of men and women and development of policies to respond to the findings (Paragraph 82l.).[10]

The Outcomes Document includes predictable recommendations, echoing the PFA, for expanding employment opportunities through, for example, career development, girls' science and technical education and training and education for women (Paragraph 82i.).[11]

A number of paragraphs address various aspects of legal guarantees for women's economic rights. In recognition of the complex nature of women's employment problems, the document calls for removing "structural and legal barriers," but also stereotypical attitudes to women's employment (Paragraph 82a).[12] It reaffirms the need for action to promote equal pay for work of equal value.

In an important breakthrough, the document calls for respect, promotion and realization of the principles contained in the ILO Declaration on Fundamental Principles and Rights at Work (Paragraph 94b.).[13] Although this falls short of a call for the ratification of the Principles that NGOs had pressed for, it still represents an advance over the PFA. Secondly, governments, for what is perhaps the first time, called for the protection of the human rights of *all* migrant women. They also called for policies to address the special needs of documented migrant women and to address inequalities between migrant women and men (Paragraph 98b).[14]

### Data

The Outcomes Document carries forward the PFA concern for gender disaggregated data to facilitate policy making. Governments of developing countries resisted proposals for international initiative and oversight of data gathering, clearly preferring that determination of data gathering priorities be strictly at the national level. The call is for international assistance, when requested, to help national governments in development of methods for statistics and data gathering for both program assessment and measuring the economic contributions of women and men. Although mentioned, the valuing of unpaid work did not receive the level of attention given in the PFA.

### Entrepreneurship and Microcredit

Reflecting a more balanced approach to women's economic empowerment than in the PFA, there are substantially fewer references to programs to promote self-help strategies for women. The initiatives are essentially a reiteration of language contained in the PFA.

## Sharing Family Responsibilities

Programs to assist the sharing of work and family responsibilities are called for, including the need for "family friendly policies." Programs to support the multiple roles of women in the family in its various forms are also called for (Paragraph 82c).[15]

## Other Concerns

### Resources

Exploration of sources of new public and private resources, including reduction of excessive military expenditures is called for, as was the case in the PFA.

### Women's Diversity

Rural women, refugee women, and older women are each specifically named in an action strategy. More attention is given to the situation of indigenous women than in the PFA.

## Reflections/Disappointments

In spite of some important language gains, in several key areas governments failed to agree on action recommendations to address the issues that they and NGOs have identified as challenges arising from globalization. Most glaring is the absence of any specific strategies to address the effects of privatization on women or to reverse the decline of expenditure for public services. Although gender budgeting was suggested as an encouraging development in the process of dealing with the impacts of globalization, there are no action proposals involving gender budgeting.

Governments also failed to endorse a commitment which was present in the draft of the document for the Beijing + 5 Regional Preparatory Meeting of the Economic Commission for Europe (ECE), which stated that bilateral and multilateral trade agreements and rules should respect international conventions that protect gender equality, equity and human rights. At the completion of the review process, the United States went to the extent of recording a reservation on the paragraphs on globalization, asserting that there is no connection between macro-level policy and gender equality. Given the need to address the negative impacts of trade agreements on women, this is a serious setback.

In addition to the earlier comments on debt cancellation strategies, it is disappointing that in light of the acknowledgement of the negative role of debt and debt servicing and SAPs, governments failed to take into account NGO suggestions for debt cancellation without economic and social adjustment conditionalities.

Finally, there was generalized resistance to the creation of time-bound targets. An NGO-sponsored proposal to establish year 2015 as a target date to eradicate poverty of women in all their diversity was not taken up. For a process that was initially touted as an opportunity for the creation of benchmarks and targets, the final B + 5 document, particularly in the area of economic empowerment and poverty eradication, is especially weak.

# Notes

Paragraphs Cited are taken from the Report of the Ad Hoc Committee of the Whole of the twenty-third special session of the General Assembly, Official Records, Twenty-third special session, Supplement No. 3 (A/S-23/10/Rev.1)

1. **Paragraph 35.** Globalization has presented new challenges for the fulfillment of the commitments made and the realization of the goals of the Beijing Conference. The globalization process has in some countries, resulted in policy shifts in favour of more open trade and financial flows, privatization of state-owned enterprises and in many cases lower public spending particularly on social services. This change has transformed patterns of production and accelerated technological advances in information and communication and affected the lives of women, both as workers and consumers. In a large number of countries, particularly in developing and least developed countries, these changes have also adversely impacted on the lives of women and have increased inequality. The gender impact of these changes has not been systematically evaluated. Globalization also has cultural, political, and social impacts affecting cultural values, lifestyles and forms of communication as well as implications for the achievement of sustainable development. Benefits of the growing global economy have been unevenly distributed leading to wider economic disparities, the feminization of poverty, increased gender inequality, including through often deteriorating work conditions and unsafe working environments especially in the informal economy and rural areas. While globalization has brought greater economic opportunities and autonomy to some women, many others have been marginalized, due to deepening inequalities among and within countries, by depriving them from the benefits of this process. Although in many countries the level of participation of women in the labour force has risen, in other cases, the application of certain economic policies have had a negative impact such that increases in women's employment often have not been matched by improvements in wages, promotions and working conditions. In many cases, women continue to be employed in low paid, part-time, and contract jobs marked by insecurity and by safety and health hazards. In many countries women, especially new entrants into the labour market, continue to be among the first to lose jobs and the last to be rehired.

    **Paragraph 36.** Increasing disparities in the economic situation among and within countries, coupled with a growing economic interdependence and dependence of States on external factors as well as the financial crises have, in recent years, altered prospects of growth and caused economic instability in many countries, with a heavy impact on the lives of women. These have affected the ability of States to provide social protection and social security as well as funding for the implementation of the Platform for Action. Such difficulties are also reflected in the shift of the cost of social protection, social security and other welfare provisions from the public sector to the household. The decreasing levels of funding available through international cooperation has contributed to further marginalization of a large number of developing countries and countries with economies in transition within which women are amongst the poorest. The agreed target of 0.7 per cent of the gross national product of developed countries for overall official development assistance has not been achieved. These factors have contributed to the increasing feminization of poverty, which has undermined efforts to achieve gender equality. Limited funding at the state-level makes it imperative that innovative approaches to the allocation of existing resources be employed, not only by Governments but also by NGOs and the private sector. One such innovation is the gender analysis of public budgets which is emerging as an important tool for determining the differential impact of expenditures on women and men to help ensure equitable use of existing resources. This analysis is crucial to promote gender equality.

2. **Paragraph 3.** The objective of the Platform for Action, which is in full conformity with the purposes and principles of the Charter of the United Nations and international law, is the empowerment of all women. The full realization of all human rights and fundamental freedoms of all women is essential for the empowerment of women. While the significance of national and regional particularities and various historical, cultural and religious backgrounds must be borne in mind, it is the duty of States, regardless of their political, economic and cultural systems, to promote and protect all human rights and fundamental freedoms. The implementation of the Platform, as well as further actions and initiatives contained in this document, including through national laws and the formulation of strategies, policies, programmes and development priorities, is the sovereign responsibility of each State, in conformity with all human rights and fundamental freedoms, and the significance of and full respect for various religious and ethical values, cultural backgrounds and philosophical convictions of individuals and their communities should contribute to the full enjoyment by women of their human rights in order to achieve equality, development and peace.

**Paragraph 4.** The Platform for Action emphasizes that women share common concerns that can be addressed only by working together and in partnership with men towards the common goal of gender equality around the world. It respects and values the full diversity of women's situations and conditions and recognizes that some women face particular barriers to their empowerment.

**Paragraph 5.** The Platform for Action recognizes that women face barriers to full equality and advancement because of such factors as their race, age, language, ethnicity, culture, religion or disability, because they are indigenous women or because of other status. Many women encounter specific obstacles related to their family status, particularly as single parents; and to their socio-economic status, including their living conditions in rural, isolated or impoverished areas. Additional barriers also exist for refugee women, other displaced women, including internally displaced women as well as for immigrant women and migrant women, including women migrant workers. Many women are also particularly affected by environmental disasters, serious and infectious diseases and various forms of violence against women.

3. The Economic Justice Caucus was a voluntary grouping of NGO representatives from around the world, which first came together during the Preparatory Meeting for the Beijing +5 Review (PrepCom) in March 2000. The Caucus worked throughout the review process to develop positions and propose language for the Outcomes Document with the aim of seeking economic justice for a diversity of women, especially the poorest.

4. **Paragraph 74c.** Continue to review, modify and implement macroeconomic and social policies and programmes, including *inter alia*, through an analysis from a gender perspective of those related to structural adjustment, external debt problems, in order to ensure women's equal access to resources and universal access to basic social services;

   **Paragraph 101a.** Take effective measures to address the challenges of globalization, including through the enhanced and effective participation of developing countries in the international economic policy decision-making process, in order to *inter alia*, guarantee the equal participation of women, in particular those from developing countries, in the process of macro-economic decision making;

   **Paragraph 101b.** Take measures with the full and effective participation of women to ensure new approaches to international development cooperation, based on stability, growth and equity with the enhanced and effective participation and the integration of developing countries in the globalizing world economy, geared towards poverty eradication and the reduction of gender-based inequality within the overall framework of achieving people centred sustainable development;

   **Paragraph 101h.** Establish, with the full and effective participation of women and in consultation with civil society, particularly NGOs, in a timely manner, social development funds, where appropriate, to alleviate the negative effects on women associated with structural adjustment programmes and trade liberalization and the disproportionate burden borne by women living in poverty;

5. **Beijing Platform for Action: Para. 358.** To facilitate implementation of the Platform for Action, interested developed and developing country partners, agreeing on a mutual commitment to allocate, on average 20 per cent of official development assistance and 20 per cent of the national budget to basic social programmes should take into account a gender perspective.

6. **Beijing Platform for Action: Para. 353.** ...Strengthening national capacities in developing countries to implement the Platform for Action will require striving for the fulfilment of the agreed target of 0.7 percent of the gross national product of developed countries for overall official development assistance as soon as possible...

7. **Paragraph 101h.** Establish, with the full and effective participation of women and in consultation with civil society, particularly NGOs, in a timely manner, social development funds, where appropriate, to alleviate the negative effects on women associated with structural adjustment programmes and trade liberalization and the disproportionate burden borne by women living in poverty;

8. **Paragraph 74b.** Create and ensure equal access to social protection systems, taking into account the specific needs of all women living in poverty, demographic changes and changes in society, to provide safeguards against the uncertainties and changes in conditions of work associated with globalization and strive to ensure that new, flexible and emerging forms of work are adequately covered by social protection;

9. **Paragraph 75.** Facilitate employment for women through *inter alia* promotion of adequate social protection, simplification of administrative procedures, removal of fiscal obstacles, where appropriate, and other measures, such as access to risk capital, credit schemes, micro credit and other funding, facilitating the establishment of micro enterprises and small and medium enterprises;

    **Paragraph 82f.** Take action to increase women's participation and to bring about a balanced representation of women and men in all sectors and occupations in the labour market, among others by encouraging the creation or expansion of institutional networks to support the career development and promotion of women;

10. **Paragraph 82l.** Analyze and respond, as necessary, to the major reasons why men and women may be affected differently by the process of job creation and retrenchment associated with economic transition and structural transformation of the economy, including globalization;

11. **Paragraph 82i.** Encourage and support the education of girls in science, mathematics, new technologies including information technologies, and technical subjects and encourage women, including through career advising to seek employment in high growth and high wage sectors and jobs;

12. **Paragraph 82a.** Promote and protect the rights of women workers and take action to remove structural and legal barriers as well as stereotypical attitudes to gender equality at work, addressing *inter alia*: gender bias in recruitment; working conditions; occupational segregation and harassment; discrimination in social protection benefits; women's occupational health and safety; unequal career opportunities and inadequate sharing, by men, of family responsibilities;

13. **Paragraph 94b.** Respect, promote and realize the principles contained in the ILO Declaration on Fundamental Principles and Rights at Work and its follow-up and strongly consider ratification and full implementation of ILO Conventions which are particularly relevant to ensure women's rights at work;

14. **Paragraph 98b.** Promote and protect the human rights of all migrant women and implement policies to address the specific needs of documented migrant women and, where necessary, tackle the existing inequalities between men and women migrants to ensure gender equality;

15. **Paragraph 82c.** Develop or strengthen policies and programmes to support the multiple roles of women in contributing to the welfare of the family in its various forms, which acknowledge the social significance of maternity and motherhood, parenting, the role of parents and legal guardians in the upbringing of children and caring for other family members. Such policies and programmes should also promote shared responsibility of parents, women and men and society as a whole in this regard;

## Liberation

We are all mothers,
and we have that fire in us,
of powerful women
whose spirits are so angry
we can laugh beauty into life
and still make you taste
the salt tears of our knowledge.
For we are not tortured
anymore;
we have seen beyond your lies and disguises,
and we have mastered the language of words,
and have mastered speech
And yes
we have also seen ourselves.
We have stripped ourselves raw
and naked piece by piece, until our flesh lies flayed
with blood on our own hands.
What terrible thing can you do us
which we have not done to ourselves?
What can you tell us
Which we didn't deceive ourselves with
a long time ago?
You cannot know how long we cried
until we laughed
over the broken pieces of our dreams.
Ignorance
shattered us into such fragments
we had to unearth ourselves piece by piece,
to recover with our own hands such unexpected relics
even we wondered
how we could hold such treasure.
Yes, we have conceived
to force our mutilated hopes
into the substance of visions
beyond your imaginings
to declare through pain our deliverance:
So do not even ask,
do not ask what it is we are labouring with this time;
Dreamers remember their dreams
When they are disturbed–
And you shall not escape
what we will make
of the broken pieces of our lives.

*Abena P.A. Busia is on the faculty of the Departments of English and Women's Studies at Rutgers University. Her poetry has been published widely around the world.*

*This poem was inspired by a conference on Black women writers that took place in Montclair, New Jersey in December 1982, at which both Gwendolyn Brooks and Toni Cade Bambara read from their work.*

*©Abena P.A. Busia. Reprinted by permission of author.*

# Appendix

## APPENDIX A
# Women 2000: A Symposium on Future Directions for Human Rights
## PROGRAM

**Coordinated by**
Center for Women's Global Leadership, Rutgers, The State University of New Jersey

**Host**
Center for the Study of Human Rights, Columbia University

**Co-sponsors**
The Center for Reproductive Law & Policy; the Law and Policy Project at Joseph L. Mailman School of Public Health, Columbia University; MADRE; Human Rights Institute, Columbia Law School; and United Nations Development Fund for Women (UNIFEM)

**Collaborating Organizations**
Akina Mama wa Afrika-London Women's Centre; Alliances for Africa; Amnesty International; Amnesty International/USA; Asia Pacific Forum on Women, Law and Development; Asian Centre for Women's Human Rights; Asian Women's Human Rights Council; Assembly of First Nations; B.a.B.e; BAOBAB for Women's Human Rights; Centro de la Mujer Peruana Flora Tristán; Development Alternatives with Women for a New Era; Equality Now; Feminist Majority Foundation; Fiji Women's Crisis Centre; FXB Center for Health and Human Rights; Human Rights Watch/Women's Rights Division; INFORM; International Alert; The International Gay and Lesbian Human Rights Commission; International Human Rights Law Group; International Women's Health Coalition; International Women's Human Rights Law Clinic- CUNY Law School; International Women's Rights Action Watch; International Women's Rights Action Watch-Asia Pacific; International Women's Tribune Centre; ISIS International Manila; ISIS-Women's International Cross-Cultural Exchange; ISIS Internacional Santiago; Jacob Blaustein Institute for the Advancement of Human Rights; Kensington Welfare Rights Union; Latin American and Caribbean Women's Health Network; Masimanyane Women's Support Centre; The National Women's Information Center-OSKA; Profamilia–Colombia; Research, Action & Information Network; Sister Namibia; United Methodist Office at the UN; WILD for Women's Human Rights; Women's Caucus for Gender Justice; Women's Environment & Development Organization; Women, Ink.; Women's International League for Peace and Freedom; Women in Law and Development in Africa; Women's Learning Partnership; Women and Media Collective; Women Living Under Muslim Laws; Women for Women's Human Rights/Kadinin Insan Haklari Projesi.

**Advisory Committee***
Edna Aquino, Amnesty International; Elena Arengo, MADRE; A. Widney Brown, Human Rights Watch/Women's Rights Division; Roxanna Carrillo, UNIFEM; Bisi Adeleye Fayemi, Akina Mama wa Afrika; Kathy Hall-Martinez, Center for Reproductive Law and Policy; Lynn Freedman, Law and Policy Project, Joseph L. Mailman School of Public Health, Columbia University; Ilana Landsberg-Lewis, UNIFEM; Ali Miller, Law and Policy Project, Joseph L. Mailman School of Public Health, Columbia University; Madeleine Rees, Office of the High Commissioner for Human Rights; Cynthia Rothschild, International Gay and Lesbian Human Rights Commission; Donna Sullivan, NYU School of Law.
*Organizational affiliation is listed for identification purposes only.*

**Staff**
Co-Producers: Cynthia Mellon and Linda Posluszny.
Charlotte Bunch; Lisa Clarke; Jewel N. Daney; Diana Gerace; Claudia Hinojosa; elmira Nazombe; Mia Roman; Lucy Vidal.
Interns: Amy Bain; Isabelle Barker; Jessica Bates; Bojana Blagojevic; Karen Cervas, Jacqueline Emery; Katie McGivern.

## APPENDIX B
# Summary of Center for Women's Global Leadership's Beijing + 5 Activities

THE PRIMARY GOAL OF THE WORK OF THE CENTER FOR WOMEN'S Global Leadership (Global Center) during the Beijing + 5 review was to advance a feminist human rights perspective, as spelled out in the Working Paper on a Human Rights Based Approach to the Beijing + 5 Review (see Appendix D). To do this, the Center was engaged in a range of monitoring, mobilizing and educational activities throughout 1999–2000, working with a variety of partners nationally, regionally and internationally. While the Center was concerned with implementation and human rights accountability for all aspects of the Beijing Platform for Action, its work focused primarily on the following: globalization and economic justice; violence against women in all its forms; human rights instruments and gender mainstreaming; and recognizing diversity and discrimination against marginalized women.

### Rights Based Analysis of the Beijing + 5 Review
The Global Center participated in many panels and events in which it presented its approach to the review. A working paper was prepared and distributed widely, which outlined a feminist rights based approach to the Beijing + 5 review and beyond. These ideas also served as the starting point for a global discussion on the Human Rights chapter of the Beijing Platform, which the Global Center facilitated as part of the Women Watch online working group, "Claim Women's Human Rights" (November 8–December 17, 1999). The working paper was revised and used at the Economic Commission for Europe (ECE) and the Economic Commission for Latin America and the Caribbean (ECLAC) regional meetings, and at the final preparatory session for the Beijing + 5 review.

### Provision of Information and Participation in NGO Coordination
The Global Center sought to be a reliable source of information for women around the world about the Beijing + 5 process. This was done primarily through the website and by sending regular updates and alerts to the women's human rights community. The Center also participated in a variety of efforts to help coordinate and enhance NGO participation throughout the process,

which included being part of the CONGO-initiated NGO International Coordinating Committee and the U.S. NGO Host Committee. The Center participated in many meetings and convened a number of strategy discussions about Beijing + 5 with women's human rights activists.

**Monitoring and Advocacy**
The Global Center monitored plans for and was active at the Commission on the Status of Women Preparatory Meetings (PrepComs) for the UNGASS held in March 1999 and March 2000, and at the Special Session in June 2000. The Center convened the human rights caucus at these events and co-convened the economic justice and globalization caucus. It helped to convene the Women's International Coalition for Economic Justice retreat and related activities. The Center also participated in caucuses in the areas of violence against women, young women, and health and sexual rights. Together with the Women's Environment and Development Organization (WEDO), the Center co-sponsored the Linkage Caucus, which sought to bring together work on all the issues of the Beijing Platform. The Linkage Caucus helped to form the Coalition in Support of the Beijing Platform for Action, which encompassed over 500 groups working to advance the Platform. Throughout the year, the Center also worked with a number of groups, locally and internationally, to monitor the negotiations on the document that took place at UN informal sessions and other special meetings.

**Advocacy at the ECE Regional Meeting (January 19–21, 2000, Geneva)**
The Global Center actively participated in the ECE Regional meeting and worked with other women's human rights advocates to ensure the strongest possible commitment to women's human rights in the proceedings of the ECE. The Center convened the NGO Caucus on Violence Against Women and was active in the Caucus on the Economy. It also sponsored workshops that focused on these themes from a human rights perspective.

**Advocacy at the ECLAC Regional Meeting (February 5-10, 2000, Lima)**
The Center sent representatives to the Latin American and Caribbean regional meeting, where they networked and worked with women to coordinate women's human rights strategies for Beijing + 5. Activities included participation in an orientation session at which the Center provided an update on the UN negotiations in New York, translation of materials—including the working paper on a human rights based approach to the review, and statements gener-

ated at the meeting—and generally sharing strategies that were emerging from the different regional meetings.

### Beijing + 5 Monitoring and Advocacy in the U.S.
The Global Center joined other U.S.-based NGOs in advocating a strong rights based approach by the U.S. government to the Beijing + 5 review. Through its alerts, website, media outreach and speaking engagements, the Center encouraged the broad participation of U.S. women's groups in "bringing Beijing home" by assessing the U.S. government's record of meeting its commitments to the Beijing Platform. The Center participated in one of the U.S. regional preparatory meetings for Beijing + 5, which was held in Delaware on November 6, 1999, where it led workshops on Women and the Economy and Women and Decision-Making.

### Women's Human Rights Symposium and NGO activities at the UNGASS
The Global Center sponsored or co-sponsored a number of parallel NGO events during the week of the UNGASS special session, focusing primarily on the areas of emphasis of its work, as outlined above. These included a half-day popular education training on women in the global economy, a panel on women and poverty, and sessions on sexual rights. The centerpiece of the Center's activities was "Women 2000: A Symposium on Future Directions for Human Rights." The symposium, which was attended by 1,300 people, provided an opportunity for public reflection on women's human rights advocacy over the past ten years. It included a panel on visions and challenges for the future and presentations that highlighted innovative strategies from around the world which were aimed at implementing women's human rights locally. Held on the eve of the Special Session (June 4), the symposium also served as an occasion for women to declare their determination to defend the Beijing Platform for Action and to discuss the movement's work for its implementation.

## APPENDIX C
# Women Prepare for the Beijing + 5 Review

*Susana Fried and Charlotte Bunch*

During the year 2000, the UN will review progress on implementation of the Beijing Platform for Action through what has come to be called the "Plus 5" review process. There will be regional meetings in the five UN regions, a second international Preparatory Committee during the Commission on the Status of Women (CSW) annual session in New York, 28 February–17 March, 2000 and a Special Session of the General Assembly, entitled "Women 2000: Gender Equality, Development and Peace for the 21st Century," in New York, June 5-9, 2000. While this is NOT a UN World Conference, it is an important time for activists to question what their governments have done at the national level as well as to monitor what governments and the UN claim to have done internationally.

## Background

The first preparatory committee (PrepCom) for the fifth year review was held from March 15-19, 1999, as an added week to the CSW's annual session. Delegates adopted an "enabling" resolution, which sets the basic framework for the review, including the preparatory process, the format and structure of the session, the substantive content/structure of the review, and the rules of participation. The resolution, "Preparations for the Special Session of the General Assembly entitled 'Women 2000: Gender Equality, Development and Peace for the Twenty-First Century'" is available on-line at http://www.un.org/womenwatch/daw/csw/enabling.htm.

For the PrepCom, the Secretariat (UN Division for the Advancement of Women) distributed a series of background documents, including a report of the Secretary-General entitled: *Framework for further actions and initiatives that might be considered during the special session of the General Assembly entitled "Women 2000: gender equality, development and peace for the twenty-first century."* This document (E/CN.6/1999/PC/2 hereafter referred to as PC/2) set out recommendations for the content of the review and proposed a framework along five functional categories which are still under consideration:

a. Political will and commitment to creating an enabling environment for implementation of the Platform for Action;
b. Capacity-building for advancement of women and gender mainstreaming;
c. Accountability for and assessment of the implementation of the strategies and actions in the Platform for Action;
d. Cooperation and partnership for implementing the Platform for Action;
e. Assistance to women and girls currently subject to discrimination and disadvantage.

This document also proposed four cross-cutting themes: 1. Globalization and the economic empowerment of women, especially poor women; 2. Women, science and technology and the new information age; 3. Women's leadership; and 4. Human security and social protection to form the main work of the CSW following the fifth year review. After some discussion of the themes and their relationship to the 12 critical areas of concern, it was decided that further elaboration of themes and emerging issues should happen at the regional meetings and be finalized at the March 2000 PrepCom.

**Preparatory Process**

In October 1998, the Division for the Advancement of Women (DAW), distributed a questionnaire to governments regarding implementation of the Beijing Platform for Action (PFA). Reports will be prepared based on the responses to these questions, along with an analysis of national action plans, reports submitted by States parties to the Committee on the Elimination of Discrimination Against Women (CEDAW), statistics available from various UN sources, and information generated since 1995 in the review of implementation conducted by the CSW. The enabling resolution **invites** Member States to submit their responses to the questionnaire and "to report on good practices, positive actions, lessons learned, the use of qualitative and quantitative indicators for measuring progress wherever possible, key challenges remaining in the critical areas of concern of the Platform for Action and obstacles encountered." In addition, governments that have not yet done so, are **invited** to prepare and submit national action plans on implementation of the PFA, with the participation of civil society. To date 113 Member States, one Observer and five Interregional, regional and subregional groups have submitted plans to DAW. These plans can be accessed on-line at http://www.un.org/womenwatch/followup/national/natplans.htm.

NGOs should find out what their governments are doing to respond to the questionnaires, press to be involved in any plans for reporting and consider doing alternative reports. Some NGOs at the CSW developed recommendations for NGO "alternative" reports at the national as well as regional and global level. The basis for these "alternative" reports would be the questionnaire to governments, but would extend beyond the questionnaire to include relevant information about advances and retreats in the status of women, in line with the strategic objectives in the 12 critical areas of concern of the PFA.

The resolution also encourages all the UN regional commissions to carry out activities in support of the Special Session, and regional meetings are being planned for late 1999 and early 2000. NGOs need to get involved in the regional meetings as they can influence the global process as well as provide sites for planning and accountability regionally. Contact your women's and/or foreign affairs ministries about their plans and ensure that the meetings provide for substantial NGO involvement.

**Format and Rules of the Special Session**

Governments agreed that the Special Session will have a Plenary and an Ad Hoc Committee of the Whole. This parallel session format provides the potential for greater NGO participation in the debates, particularly in the Ad Hoc Committee of the Whole, in which the rules of procedure are set by the Chair. However, the "modalities" (whether we can speak and how) for NGO participation were deferred until the next PrepCom in March 2000.

Regarding NGO access to the Session, it was decided that "NGOs in consultative status with the Economic and Social Council (ECOSOC) and NGOs accredited to the Fourth World Conference on Women (FWCW) may participate in the Special Session." NGOs sought to get "NGOs applying for ECOSOC status" included as a third category that provided for newer groups that have been formed since the FWCW. This issue can be re-opened at the PreCom in March 2000. If you have questions about whether your organization can be accredited to the PrepCom or the Special Session, contact Koh Miyaoi, Division for the Advancement of Women, fax: (1-212) 963-3463, e-mail: daw@un.org.

**Substantive Content/Structure of the Review**

The provisional agenda for the Special Session includes: review and appraisal of progress made in the implementation of the 12 critical areas of concern in the PFA; and other actions and initiatives for overcoming obstacles to implementation of the PFA. *The resolution reaffirms the PFA and notes that there will be no renegotiation of the existing agreements.* The Special Session will also consider recommendations for accelerated implementation of the PFA taking into consideration the Secretary-General's report of further actions contained in PC/2. The Secretary-General has been asked to prepare comprehensive reports in time for the PrepCom in March 2000 on the implementation of the Platform for Action nationally, regionally and internationally, based on the governmental reports mentioned above and taking into account all relevant information and inputs available to the UN system.

NGOs monitoring the framework for the review emphasized the importance of maintaining a clear link to the 12 critical areas of concern, a focus on accelerated implementation and a clear discussion of accountability. NGOs proposed that the document that comes out of the review should be structured around actions to accelerate implementation and address obstacles. Further, many NGOs emphasized that the structure and content of the review should be discussed widely in broad consultation, based in particular on the regional meetings. The themes of action, concrete benchmarks for progress, and accountability need to be continuously emphasized throughout this process.

## Parallel NGO Activities and NGO Coordination

A range of discussions took place during the PrepCom about NGO coordination and activities that might take place immediately prior to, or during, the PrepCom and the Special Session. It was emphasized that while there should be some NGO parallel events, the focus of NGO activity should be aimed directly at affecting the Inter-governmental session. *There will not be an NGO Forum similar to those at World Conferences as this is not a World Conference.* CONGO (the body comprised of NGOs in consultative status with ECOSOC) will help coordinate these activities, in collaboration with issue-based caucuses, global networks and regional groupings, among others. NGOs at the CSW agreed that a Coordinating Committee should be formed to facilitate communication and coordination of parallel activities, and of key points for NGO advocacy around the Special Session. These plans are in an early stage of development, under the leadership of CONGO.

Another group met during the PrepCom to discuss the use of electronic networking and proposed that a global web site be constructed as a resource for the review process that would incorporate existing regional and thematic websites, along with other existing resources, such as the Womenwatch website (http://www.un.org/womenwatch) produced by the UN Division for the

Advancement of Women, UNIFEM and INSTRAW. For more information about the NGO website, contact WomenAction 2000 at wimnet@gn.apc.org.

The **Center for Women's Global Leadership** will continue monitoring discussions among governments and NGOs regarding the Beijing + 5 Review. We will be working with other groups concerned with women's human rights to discuss how these issues will be reviewed throughout the process—nationally, regionally and globally. We will send out periodic updates and provide more information on our activities as they develop. A summary of our plans can be viewed on the Center's website, http://www.cwgl.rutgers.edu.

The Center for Women's Global Leadership will also monitor a series of global discussions held on-line that will focus on a feminist rights-based approach to the Beijing review and beyond. These discussions will begin with the **Claim Women's Human Rights** discussion on Womenwatch, http://www.un.org/womenwatch (8 November 1999–17 December 1999) and will continue on WhrNet, http://www.whrnet.org, throughout the review process.

## APPENDIX D
# Working Paper on a Human Rights Based Approach to the Beijing + 5 Review

*Center for Women's Global Leadership, February 2000*

## Introduction

THE FIVE YEAR REVIEW OF THE BEIJING PLATFORM FOR ACTION (Beijing + 5) presents an important opportunity to advance implementation of the Platform and the promotion of women's human rights. During the 1990s, women's human rights advocates achieved recognition that women's rights are human rights. The language of protecting and promoting the human rights of women has been widely incorporated into the rhetoric of governments and inter-governmental organizations. Yet reality lags far behind such rhetoric. Concerted action and the allocation of resources required to effectively reduce and ultimately put an end to human rights violations against women have not yet been committed.

This review must affirm the Beijing Platform for Action as a human rights based document. The Platform is one of the most comprehensive expressions of governments' commitments to human rights for women and girls based on the understanding that women's rights are human rights. Its detailed proposals begin to give concrete shape to the human rights of women in all twelve critical areas of concern. When taken together with the human rights conventions—the Universal Declaration of Human Rights, the International Covenant on Economic, Social and Cultural Rights, the International Covenant on Civil and Political Rights, CEDAW and others—as well as the documents of the other UN conferences of this decade—the World Conference on Human Rights, the International Conference on Population and Development, the World Summit for Social Development, the World Summit for Children, the Second UN Conference on Human Settlements, and the Conference on Environment and Development—it provides a substantial vision and strategies for the next decade.

The Beijing + 5 Review is not, therefore, about abstract concepts. Discriminatory laws and other violations of women's human rights affect the lives and cause the deaths of women and girls every day. It is essential that this review seek ways to accelerate implementation of the Platform along with ways of measuring progress towards its stated goals. The Platform for Action notes that "unless the human rights of women, as defined by international human rights instruments, are fully recognized and effectively protected, applied, implemented and enforced in national law as well as national practice in family, civil, penal, labor and commercial codes and administrative rules and regulations, they will exist in name only" (Paragraph 218).

The question now is how best to use this year 2000 review as a springboard to move forward and to get governments and the UN to take more concrete steps to advance the human rights of women. A feminist human rights based approach to implementing the Platform for Action and gaining women's rights more generally can be useful here. A feminist analysis places women—in all their diversity—at the center of the agenda. It evaluates all policies, practices and actions for their real or potential effect on women's lives, taking into account the multiple intersections of race, class, age, ethnicity, sexual orientation, religious affiliation, access to income and types of physical and mental abilities.

Two of the most important aspects of a rights-based approach are standard setting and accountability. The human rights conventions provide an ethical perspective and set common standards for achievement that serve as yardsticks for all peoples and all nations to promote respect for the rights and freedoms of all. Accountability means that it is not merely a good idea, but that it is a duty of governments, the United Nations and other inter-governmental bodies to make every effort to implement the human rights commitments they have made. Since governments are responsible for implementing human rights standards, they must live up to them themselves and they must implement them in relation to others: the private sector—including corporations and other bodies for which governments hold regulatory responsibility—and private individuals over whose conduct governments carry judicial responsibility.

Accountability to implementation can be more effectively determined by setting out goals and targets nationally, regionally and internationally. While the Beijing Platform for Action is one of the most visionary of the 1990s world conferences, it contains little in the way of specific targets and benchmarks, in contrast to some of the other world conferences. It is time to develop specific targets along with time lines and indicators by which progress can be measured.

One essential element in meeting targets for implementation of the Beijing Platform is the allocation of adequate resources. While the issue of resources presents difficulties for many governments, creative ways of reallocating existing resources as well as strategies for generating new ones must be found if the Platform is to go beyond good rhetoric. Strategies for more effective ways that resources can be deployed for making women's human rights a reality include:

using gender audits for budgets to make sure all programs are gender sensitive; making more effective use of existing resources to reflect gender-sensitive priorities; and ensuring that funds reach women at the grassroots. Unwillingness to address this question of resources reveals a lack of political will to work for gender equality and the promotion of women's human rights.

One of the minimum expressions of political will is legislation that makes the violation of women's human rights illegal, along with removing discriminatory laws from all national codes. Another expression of political will is the gathering of comprehensive data that is disaggregated by gender and that draws on the work of NGOs and grassroots women's groups. Such data can form the basis for more effective policies and can be used to formulate benchmarks and indicators of progress. The data which has been gathered by women for many years must be taken into account and utilized in this process.

This document looks at two of the areas that will be addressed by governments during the review process: violence against women and women's economic rights. It represents part of the Global Center's efforts to promote a human rights based approach to all of the critical areas of concern.

## Recommendations for Action: Violence against Women

Violence against women is recognized in the World Conference on Human Rights Vienna Programme of Action and in the Beijing Platform for Action as a fundamental violation of human rights. Thus, governments have acknowledged that it is their duty to work for its elimination in all spheres of life. Violence is often an obstacle to women and girls' achievement of their human rights in all the other areas of the Platform as well. Yet, while there is considerable agreement on the goal of ending such violence, little progress has been made toward this end. In some cases, legislation is not commensurate with the seriousness of this crime, and in most cases, inadequate resources have been devoted to this problem.

The Beijing Platform sets out a significant number of specific steps that governments must take to end violence against women in the family, the community and by the state. Further, efforts to end violence must be seen as interrelated with other areas of the Platform since a woman's economic, political and social situation as well as factors such as her race, class, age, sexual orientation, ethnicity, religion, physical or mental ability, or her status as a refugee, migrant or prisoner often affect her experience of violence and her ability to escape it.

Actions to end violence against women need to be taken in many areas. Services that are comprehensive, readily available and responsive to all women in diverse settings are essential and Education/Prevention strategies are the only hope for change in the future. The following recommendations focus on the areas of Legislation/Criminal Justice, Resources and the collection of Data/Research.

**Legislation/Criminal Justice**

Legislation serves as one minimum standard of a government's commitment and political will to act against this crime. Yet, while a number of government's have adopted legislation that addresses violence against women, the crucial factor is effective enforcement of those laws, which is lagging far behind. Further, since all people are equal before the law, all forms of violence against women must be prosecuted, including those committed by partners or family members.

1. Governments must challenge and repeal all legislation that discriminates against women.
2. Governments must ensure that violence against women and children in the home and family, including marital rape, incest, forced marriages, so-called honor killings and elder abuse are treated as crimes.
3. Governments must develop clear and comprehensive guidelines for the criminal justice system and provide training to police, prosecutors and judges about their human rights obligations and the importance of gender sensitivity in handling crimes of violence against women.

**Data/Research**

It is difficult to establish benchmarks and measure progress made toward the goal of diminishing and eliminating violence against women because the data on the extent and nature of the different forms of violence is rudimentary, uneven and not based upon uniform standards and indicators. Since accurate data is a fundamental tool for effective policy formulation and allocation of resources, there is an urgent need for greater international cooperation and national attention to this problem.

1. Governments need to develop and share indicators for all types of violence against women and use them to gather more comprehensive data as well as to monitor changes in the magnitude and forms of such violence.
2. The United Nations should convene a high level international task force to develop an international consensus on uniform indicators and ways to measure violence against women.

3. The United Nations should establish a readily accessible database on statistics, legislation, training models, good practices, ethical guidelines, lessons learned and other resources with regard to all forms of violence against women.

**Resources**

To end violence against women and to enable women and children to escape violence, resources have to be allocated and increased in a number of ways. Governments need to invest more in the direct services that victims need, whether they provide these or rely on NGOs to perform them. Resources are also crucial to prevention and education as well as for accurate collection of data and the gathering of effective research on what strategies work best. The Commission on the Status of Women, in its review of the chapter of the Platform on violence against women in 1998, addressed this topic extensively in its Agreed Conclusions. Section II of those conclusions on "Provision of resources to combat violence against all women" contains useful suggestions that should be reinforced by the Beijing + 5 Review. In particular:

1. Provide adequate resources for women's groups, helplines, crisis centres and other support services, including credit, medical, psychological and other counselling services, as well as focus on vocational skill training for women victims of violence that enables them to find a means of subsistence.
2. Encourage and fund the training of personnel in the administration of justice, law enforcement agencies, security personnel, social and health care services, schools and migration authorities on matters related to gender-based violence, its prevention and the protection of women from violence.
3. Include in national budgets adequate resources related to the elimination of violence against women and girls.

**Recommendations for Action: Women and the Economy**

Women's labor, paid and unpaid, in the home, the community and the workplace, is central to the functioning of society and economy. Women of the regions are increasingly involved in the labor force. The strategic manipulation of flexible women's labor is being used to maximize economic competitiveness and to enhance profitability. The quality, level of remuneration and safety of their jobs is the central issue.

If governments are to fulfill their commitments to women's economic rights and economic empowerment, these contributions must be recognized and acknowledged and the disproportionate and gender specific impacts of economic policies must be enumerated.

Governments and the United Nations should consider the following actions to ensure women's economic rights and realization of full human dignity.

**To ensure women's rights to social protection:**
1. Governments should review employment trends to identify areas of growth of female employment (especially part time, temporary, home-based work, etc.) and the existing structures of social protection (unemployment compensation, health care, pension) to determine if women are receiving adequate and equal protection.
2. Governments, in consultation with women's organizations, should set goals for the eradication of poverty, including timelines for increases in minimum wage and public assistance programs to ensure wage levels and assistance are above the poverty line.

**To ensure women's rights to an adequate standard of living:**
1. Governments should establish legal prohibitions of discriminatory treatment of women in downsizing, plant closure, offshore industrial location, and other such practices. The United Nations and the International Labour Organization (ILO) should take leadership in opening international dialogue among the private sector, governments and civil society—especially women workers' organizations to: (1) establish ways to mitigate the negative effects of such corporate actions; and (2) establish minimum standards to guarantee sustainable livelihoods for workers in all countries, thus minimizing the competitive advantage of lowest wages.
2. Governments should advise women's organizations on the possible use of the CEDAW Optional Protocol to seek redress for the discriminatory impact of corporate policies, such as downsizing, plant closure and outsourcing.
3. National governments should organize consultations with disadvantaged women—women on welfare, grassroots and poor women, immigrant women, women with disabilities, racial and ethnic minorities, among others—to hear their views on the impacts of globalization and possible alternative strategies. People and communities should not have to bear the cost of economic injustice that centers around corporate greed.

4. Governments and the UN, in consultation with women's organizations, should study the gender impacts of free trade policies with a view to what international measures must be taken. For example:
   a. Creation of accountability indicators for transnational corporations operating in multiple countries to ensure consistency and fairness in treatment of workers;
   b. Open dialogue among the UN, the ILO and the WTO on the conduct of transnational corporations towards workers.
5. National gender machineries, in concert with NGOs, should develop criteria for Gender Impact Statements, following the model of the Structural Adjustment Participatory Review (SAPRI) initiative, in which local NGOs participate in impact audits of World Bank programs.
6. Governments should establish special initiatives for microcredit and small-scale projects that grow out of and support community needs and strategies.

# Center for Women's Global Leadership Publications

**Books**

Holding on to the Promise: Women's Human Rights and the Beijing + 5 Review (2001)

Los derechos de las mujeres son derechos humanos: Crónica de una movilización mundial (2000)

Les voix des femmes et « les droits de l'homme » (2000)

Written Out: How Sexuality is Used to Attack Women's Organizing (2000)

Local Action/Global Change: Learning About the Human Rights of Women and Girls (1999)

Without Reservation: The Global Tribunal on Accountability for Women's Human Rights (1996)

From Vienna to Beijing: The Copenhagen Hearing on Economic Justice and Women's Human Rights (1995)

From Vienna to Beijing: The Cairo Hearing on Reproductive Health and Human Rights (1994)

Demanding Accountability: The Global Campaign and Vienna Tribunal for Women's Human Rights (1994)

Testimonies of the Global Tribunal on Violations of Women's Human Rights (1994)

**Pamphlet Series**

Lesbians Travel the Roads of Feminism Globally/ La travesía de las mujeres lesbianas por el feminismo internacional (2000)

Migrant Women's Human Rights in G-7 Countries: Organizing Strategies (1997)

With Liberty and Justice for All: Women's Human Rights in the United States (1994)

Gender Violence and Women's Human Rights in Africa: A Symposium (1994)

Gender Violence: A Human Rights and Development Issue (1991)

Violencia de Género: Un Problema de Desarrollo y Derechos Humanos (1991)

La Violence Faite Aux Femmes: Une Question de Développement et de Droits Humains (1991)

**Women's Global Leadership Institute Reports**

Feminism in the Muslim World Leadership Institutes (2001)

The Indivisibility of Women's Human Rights: A Continuing Dialogue (1995)

The International Campaign for Women's Human Rights 1992-1993 Report (1993)

Women, Violence and Human Rights: 1991 Leadership Institute Report (1992)

Informe del Instituto de Liderazgo de la Mujer: Mujer, Violencia y Derechos Humanos (1992)

*For additional information about any of these publications, please visit the Center's website: www.cwgl.rutgers.edu*

**Videos**

The Vienna Tribunal: Women's Rights are Human Rights! (1993)

*For ordering information contact:*

| *In the USA:* | *Outside the USA:* | *In Spanish:* |
|---|---|---|
| Women Make Movies | Augusta Productions | SERPAJ-Mexico |
| 462 Broadway, 5th Floor | 54 Mullock St. | Ignacio Mariscal 132 |
| New York, NY 10013 USA | St. John's NFLD | Colonia Tabacalera |
| Ph: (1-212)925-0606 | CANADA A1C2RB | Mexico, D.F. 06030 |
| Fax: (1-212)925-2052 | Ph: (1-709)753-1861 | Ph: (52-5)705-0646 |
| | Fax: (1-709)579-8090 | Fax: (52-5)7-5-0771 |

## About the Editor

**Cynthia Meillón** is a writer and translator with a special interest in economic justice and women's human rights. Much of her work has focused on the effects of multilateral trade agreements and globalization on women and their communities. She was formerly editor of *Beyond Law/Más Allá del Derecho*—a journal of law and social change published in Bogotá, Colombia. She spent 1999-2000 monitoring the Beijing + 5 process with the Center for Women's Global Leadership.

## The Center for Women's Global Leadership (Global Center)

Develops and facilitates women's global leadership toward women's human rights and social justice worldwide. The Center's programs promote the leadership of women and advance feminist perspectives in policy-making processes in local, national and international arenas. Since 1990, the Global Center has fostered women's leadership in the area of human rights through women's global leadership institutes, strategic planning activities, international mobilization campaigns, UN monitoring, global education endeavors, publications and a resource center. The Center works from a human rights perspective with an emphasis on violence against women, sexual and reproductive rights and socio-economic well-being.

The Center's activities are based on seeing women's leadership and transformative visions as crucial in every policy area from democratization and human rights to global security and economic restructuring. Such global issues are interconnected and have both local and international dimensions. The creation of effective policy alternatives demands the full inclusion of gender perspectives and women in all decision-making processes and requires an understanding of how gender relates to race, class, ethnicity, sexual orientation and culture.

## Funders

The Ford Foundation, The John D. and Catherine T. MacArthur Foundation, The Moriah Fund, Open Society Institute, Rutgers, the State University of New Jersey, Shaler Adams Foundation, United Nations Development Fund for Women (UNIFEM).